Kayak Trips

in Puget Sound and the San Juan Islands

Kayak Trips
in Puget Sound and the San Juan Islands

by Randel Washburne

Pacific Search Press

Pacific Search Press, 222 Dexter Avenue North
    Seattle, Washington 98109
© 1986 by Randel Washburne. All rights reserved
Printed in the United States of America

Edited by Margaret Foster-Finan
Designed by Judy Petry

Maps by Judy Petry
Photographs by Randel Washburne

Cover: *Kayakers exploring the Cone Islands near Cypress Island
(Joel W. Rogers)*

Library of Congress Cataloging-in-Publication Data

Washburne, Randel.
    Kayak trips in Puget Sound and the San Juan Islands.

    Bibliography: p.
    Includes index.
    1. Canoes and canoeing—Washington (State)—Puget
Sound—Guide-books. 2. Puget Sound (Wash.)—Description—
Guide-books. 3. Canoes and canoeing—Washington—
San Juan Islands—Guide-books. 4. San Juan Islands
(Wash.)—Description—Guide-books. I. Title.
GV776.W22P848   1986   917.97 ''7   86-4985
ISBN 0-931397-05-7

Contents

Acknowledgments   7
Introduction   8

THE PUGET SOUND/SAN JUAN ISLANDS PADDLING
ENVIRONMENT   15
   Weather, Water, and Marine Shipping   17
   Tides and Currents   23
   Going Ashore   33
   Going Paddling   41

PLACES TO GO—THE SAN JUAN ISLANDS   51
   Stuart Island   52
   The Northern Rim Islands   60
      *North shore of Orcas Island, Patos Island, Sucia Island,
      Matia Island, and Clark Island*
   Lummi Island   70
   Central San Juan Islands   74
      Shaw Island, Jones Island, and Turn Island
   Western Rosario Strait   82
      Eastern Orcas Island, Blakely Island, and James Island
   Cypress Island   88

PLACES TO GO—NORTH PUGET SOUND   93
   Skagit River Delta   94
   Indian Island   100
   Everett Harbor   106
      Jetty Island and Vicinity
   Eagle Harbor   112
   Blake Island   116

PLACES TO GO—SOUTH PUGET SOUND   121
   Maury Island   122
   Nisqually Delta   128
   Carr Inlet   132
      Raft Island, Cutts Island, and Kopachuck State Park
   Hartstene Island   136

APPENDICES   143
    Table 1   144
    Table 2   146
    Equipment Checklist   147
    Useful Publications   148

    Index   151

Acknowledgments

My greatest debt of thanks takes the form of a dedication for this book—to my friend Linda Daniel. As with *The Coastal Kayaker: Kayak Camping on the Alaska and B.C. Coast*, this book simply would not exist were it not for her encouragement and advice. Her editing touch is found in many spots throughout.

To the individuals who lent their time and expertise to review portions of my manuscript, I owe particular thanks. Dr. Harold Mofjeld of NOAA has been invaluable in helping me to understand tide rips and other current-related phenomena. Dr. David Burch of Starpath School of Navigation greatly improved my coverage of weather and marine traffic hazards. Kelly Tjaden of Seaworthy Designs brought his extensive experience with paddling in the San Juan Islands to bear on my trip descriptions for that area.

Bits and pieces of information came from many individuals willing to share their local knowledge. Among them were Tim Davis, Oscar Lind, Chris Mork, Judy and Lee Moyer, Tom Meyers, Stan Reeve, Neville Richter, Bill Ross, Marian Slater, Hank Snelgrove, and Tom Steinburn. I also appreciate the companionship of those who accompanied me at different times in paddling research: Kevin Cron, Linda Daniel, Mike and Susan Huffman, Dwight Jacobson, Hank Snelgrove, Kelly Tjaden, and Bill Turner.

I was particularly concerned about including information on public facilities and services that was both accurate and consistent with management policies and I am grateful to the agencies and the individuals who lent their help. I would like to thank Dave Castor, Will Lorentz, Doug Peznecker, and Tom Snyder of the Washington State Parks; John Garrett of the Washington Department of Game; Pat Patterson and Bob Wheeler of the Washington State Ferries; and Ellie Henke of the U.S. Fish and Wildlife Service. I also owe thanks to Dave Duggins for his information on The Nature Conservancy's Yellow Island and on the University of Washington's biological preserves in the San Juan Islands.

At Pacific Search Press, I am grateful to Carolyn Threadgill for encouraging me to do this book, to Margaret Foster-Finan who first had the idea and then helped make it a reality, and to Judy Petry for the maps and graphic design.

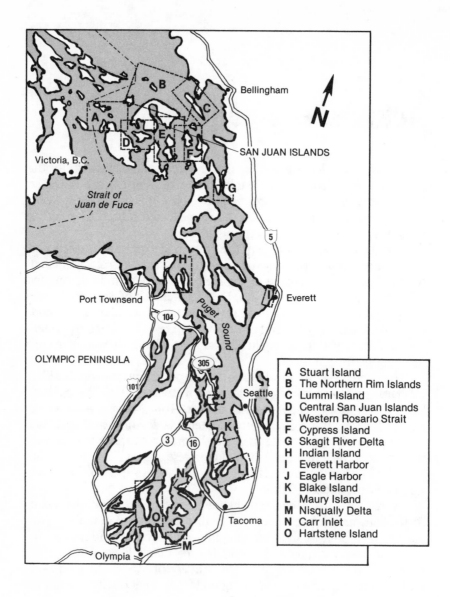

Bellingham

N

SAN JUAN ISLANDS

Victoria, B.C.

*Strait of
Juan de Fuca*

5

H

Port Townsend

Everett

104

*Puget
Sound*

OLYMPIC PENINSULA

305

101

3   16

Seattle

J

K

N

L

O

Tacoma

M

Olympia

A	Stuart Island
B	The Northern Rim Islands
C	Lummi Island
D	Central San Juan Islands
E	Western Rosario Strait
F	Cypress Island
G	Skagit River Delta
H	Indian Island
I	Everett Harbor
J	Eagle Harbor
K	Blake Island
L	Maury Island
M	Nisqually Delta
N	Carr Inlet
O	Hartstene Island

Introduction

The Pacific Northwest has a national reputation as prime boating country, and its extensive inland waterways are considered among the best in the world for sea kayaking. The attributes that make good boating of any kind also make good paddling—beautiful scenery, intricate and protected waterways, clear and clean water, abundant marine life, and a lot more. On shore there are ample public parklands, many on islands where the original wilderness charm still is strong.

The kayaker's perspective on his surroundings is a bit different from that of other boaters. And from the close-to-the-water and close-to-the-land perspective, the Pacific Northwest reveals an extra, appealing dimension.

For us "little boaters," shoreline is everything. It is along the shoreline that most of us prefer to direct our travels, rather than heading across open water. We experience it at touching distance within the intertidal zone: holding to a rock while drifting on a calm afternoon, leaning back to look straight up to the brick red trunk of a madrona against the blue sky, lingering beneath the city's piers on a quiet Sunday morn-

Rosario Strait near Strawberry Island.

ing to watch the sun illuminate the anemone-coated pilings below.

Washington's shorelines have "texture," a word that expresses all the things that make it interesting: the spongelike eroded sandstones of Sucia Island, the crumbling canneries along Guemes Channel, the tiny channels that at high tide meander inland for miles through the Nisqually Flats' marshlands. Few other boaters know this texture as kayakers do. In these places we meet the creatures that other boaters scarcely see at all: myriad sea- and shorebirds, river otters, and orcas. Kayakers share a special relationship with their most customary traveling companion, the shy but curious harbor seal, and experience such humorous aspects as the seal's embarrassment when you make eye contact with him.

Just as kayakers look to the land for enjoyment, we also look to the sea—and like how it treats us in the Pacific Northwest. Sea kayakers from the stormy, unsheltered British coast comment that paddling is so *easy* here. With our winding inland channels and frequently docile winds, that is a valid observation. At least during the warmer months, sunny highs drift in to stay for weeks, breezes are languid, and kayakers overtake sailors too stubborn to motor.

Particularly in the San Juan Islands' powerful tide races, kayaks pass the sailboats with hardly a stroke, threading behind the kelp beds in back eddies along the shores. Our currents are at once a threat and a blessing, contributing the largest part to Washington's paddling identity, with their free rides and perilous tide rips. Probably more than for any other kind of boater, the kayaker is engaged by both the positive and negative aspects of moving salt water. In the Northwest, we quickly learn the currents' workings by necessity since an opposing current can make rough seas murderous. In these waters, the whitewater paddler can find something reminiscent of the river drops back home, while the more contemplative sightseer can regard currents through streaming, swaying kelp beds on long downstream runs.

In short, saltwater kayaking hardly needs selling to Pacific Northwesterners. Thousands have already discovered its charms, and sea kayaks are becoming a significant element among the pleasure vessels cruising Washington's waterways. New kayakers come to it from diverse backgrounds. Many aficionados of self-propelled terrestrial travel—backpackers, cross-country skiers—have found in kayaks an agreeable and reasonably priced way to explore a whole new realm. Marine channels open to them like an unexplored network of trails. And, for white-water river paddlers, many skills transfer easily.

Still another group is the experienced saltwater boater who discovers the comparative simplicity of kayak travel and its special relationship to the surroundings. An ex-sailor recalls his dissatisfaction with experiences under sail—boredom liberally laced with exasper-

La Conner.

ation at our typically fluky winds. His experiences with paddle in hand
are uniformly more interesting, less sedentary, and less stressful. Other
converts speak of the new level of intimacy with the seashore that
kayaking brings.

"In the San Juans, there were so many places I'd passed countless
times, but never *seen*, being too busy worrying about staying off
enough to avoid scraping my keel. And it was just too much trouble to
anchor and go ashore. It's like I have a whole new place to explore!"

Still others revel in trading the cramped accommodations on
board for spacious campsites on shore, gladly swapping sixteen hours
of motoring from Seattle to the San Juan Islands (after waiting in line
for the Chittenden Locks) for two hours on the highway, perhaps
followed by a ferry ride. And not least, monthly loan and moorage
payments for a large boat cannot compare to a onetime, one-
thousand-dollar investment in a kayak, which stores free of charge
behind the garage.

More than a few sailors and powerboaters in Washington and
British Columbia's inland waters have found kayaks to be excellent
shore boats—either stowed on decks of larger yachts or towed behind
smaller ones. These boaters enjoy the best of both worlds—a quiet
evening of solitary paddling along shore plays counterpoint to the
challenges or sedentariness of a day under sail or power. Kayaks have
limitations as shore boats. They are poorly suited for carrying such
bulky gear as ice chests, can take only as many adults as there are

Sailboat towing kayak.

cockpits, and are tricky to get in and out of from boats without a boarding step on the transom.

Kayaks can be towed successfully by sailboats (not faster power-boats) in varying weather conditions, say many who have done so in Puget Sound and the San Juan Islands. (Though some admit not wanting that additional concern if things get nasty.) Most kayaks track well under tow (one sailor said his kayak needed its nonsteerable skeg down to do so), and are best kept empty and as light as possible. There *must* be a tightly fitting cockpit cover that will stay on if the kayak should flip. The length of the towline requires experimentation in dif-ferent conditions. One sailor brings his kayak's bow right up onto his transom in difficult following seas; he says it rides well there. Two kayaks can be towed side by side, with short poles connecting bows and sterns to keep the boats apart and in line with each other.

But this book is not about sea kayaking in general. (I mention towing kayaks because it is probably more popular among boaters in Puget Sound and the San Juan Islands than anywhere else.) The focus will be similarly confined for most aspects of saltwater paddling, that is, how they relate to this particular setting. And though the focus is on this particular region, this book is not intended to compete with the several fine guidebooks for water goers in this area (listed under Useful Publications). All of the history and much of the shore-based descrip-tions are too well documented to merit repeating. However, general boating guides often lack specific information for sea kayakers, information that other boaters find unfamiliar and perhaps even peculiar. A few of the guides include a good dose of each local sea's personality and I have tried to add those especially attractive or repulsive to kayakers. Ashore, I found a great many things of interest to kayak visitors that I have not found referenced anywhere else: which beaches are prone to freighters' surge, which campgrounds are usually full (sometimes with other kayakers), which way you should turn to launch your kayak as you stroll off the ferry at Friday Harbor or Winslow towing your boat on its cart behind you, which shore has the eddy that can get you from here to there. I also address misconceptions often held by new kayakers that lead to disappointments or sometimes trouble, such as notions of available water at a place where in fact there is none.

I describe trips to a variety of specific places. These trips are by no means all of the suitable places to have superior sea kayaking experiences along Washington's waterways, but they are among the best. I used the same criteria in selecting them as in deciding where to dip my own paddle. I focused on loop-trip possibilities so that there can be new shoreline all the way, though a few out-and-back day trips are included for their own merits. Though wild scenery is always desirable, I also picked places where development is dominant, yet attractive for its antiquity, interesting for its marine/industrial culture, or for the intricacy that over-the-water construction can sometimes present, or perhaps just as a contrast to some tiny pristine enclave. And, since most kayakers are also campers, opportunities for two- or three-day cruises with overnight stopovers are heavily represented along with day trips. I did not venture into some regions at all: the many possibilities of Hood Canal, the long coastline west through the Strait of Juan de Fuca.

Finally, with some trepidation, I rated saltwater kayak routes in this book by the degree of hazard potential. Much needed, this was as slippery a task as getting a footing on a kelp-covered rock.

All routes are rated as either **exposed**, **moderate**, or **protected**, ratings which comprise the numerous independent and sometimes ethereal elements that are the sea environment. Unlike easily rated rivers with predictable conditions that are related to a particular rate of flow, sea conditions change by minutes as winds and currents change in intensity independent of one another. My ratings are based on *potentials* for trouble that may express themselves only rarely, but perhaps with dire consequences: tide rips that spring up from nowhere when the tide changes or a sudden wind that delivers difficult seas during a crossing. There is a real danger that new sea kayakers, lulled by a placid first trip, might be drawn into traps laid by changing weather or tides with few escape routes. I am particularly concerned about week-end trips, where the demands to be home by Sunday night and the lack of a long but easy alternative route leads to "going for it" into a nasty crossing. Sucia Island and its neighboring islands are a trip frequented by the weekend neophyte kayaker (my very first overnight paddle was there), yet my criteria led me to rate it **exposed.** A kayaking fatality did occur in the vicinity in 1985. So, in spite of the patterns of kayaking use, these ratings suggest the potential for trouble, based on circum-stances and what I and others have encountered there. How you use them depends on your abilities and willingness to take chances.

You might evaluate your own ability to counter the potential sea forces according to your awareness, strength, and survival skills on the water. Awareness is your ability to anticipate and avoid hazards, for example, to spot a dangerous tide rip far downstream and assess which way to paddle to avoid it. Strength is your ability to paddle hard against wind or current to escape a bad situation. Survival skills on the water are your boat-handling reflexes (balance, braces, or rolls) that enable you to keep going in spite of the sea's energies around you (with the hope that conditions will eventually moderate or that you will reach calmer water).

In my travels around these sounds and islands, the vast majority of times have been good ones. The dangers stay well in the background of my recollections without coloring the pleasures. I hope this book can help you turn your kayak explorations of these waters into equally fond memories.

Last, I admit to taking some liberties with the names of bodies of water for the sake of simplicity, primarily the much-abused "Puget Sound," which often has been inflated to encompass all of western Washington. Technically, this waterway becomes Admiralty Inlet at Foulweather Bluff, far south of its connection with eastern Strait of Juan de Fuca and the San Juan Islands. However, in this book, Puget Sound is used loosely to mean all those waterways that meander their ways in southerly directions from the San Juan Islands environs. May the cartographers among you forgive me.

The Puget Sound/ San Juan Islands Paddling Environment

Weather, Water, and Marine Shipping

The sea-kayaking environment is always characterized by unpredictable elements, the weather being a primary offender. There are, however, consistencies that govern the changes in Northwest marine weather, just as there are rules that control the movements of ships in these waters, and means for helping kayakers stay out of trouble from both. Additionally, there is a hazard that affects sea kayakers in most nontropical waters: sea temperature. In these waters, immersion and resulting hypothermia are a problem serious enough to merit special discussion.

Marine Weather

For kayakers, the most important variable is wind and the resulting sea state. Unfortunately, winds are difficult for meteorologists to forecast, especially in the Pacific Northwest. Visual cues that you can use to predict what is coming are even less reliable, though there are a few I will take note of in this very brief treatment of Washington's marine weather. For a more thorough understanding of patterns, I strongly recommend Kenneth Lilly's book, *Marine Weather of Western Washington* (listed under Useful Publications).

The maritime Northwest's year is almost equally divided into two seasonal weather regimes, each with characteristic patterns. The two regimes are governed by two large atmospheric pressure cells. The Pacific High is always present off the California coast, but expands north in the spring to dominate the entire northeast Pacific until early fall. Then the high retreats south and is replaced by the growing Aleutian Low, which moves south in the fall from the Bering Sea to the Gulf of Alaska for the winter. In spring the low weakens and retreats to the northwest Pacific and the Bering Sea, again replaced with the high.

The summer pattern usually eases in during April and gives way in September. Gales (winds stronger than 33 knots) decrease in frequency toward midsummer as the region becomes dominated by the stable Pacific High pressure, which blocks most disturbances from entering the area. Nonetheless, lows and fronts can bring rain and strong winds, which almost always blow from a southerly direction during bad weather.

During fair weather, winds still can be quite fresh. As the interior landmass warms, air from high pressure areas in the Pacific Ocean is drawn in through the Strait of Juan de Fuca, where it can blow 25 knots or more in the afternoon. These winds spread to the north and south at the eastern end of the straits, sending southwesterlies up into the San Juan Islands and northwesterlies down across Port Townsend and into northern Puget Sound. Other than as influenced by the Strait of Juan de Fuca, winds tend to be northwesterly during fair weather in the summer regime.

Of course, topography plays an important part in wind direction and force throughout the area. Heating of land creates local onshore winds (called sea breezes) on most sunny afternoons. Hence morning is generally the least windy time for paddling. When the sea breeze direction coincides with the prevailing northwesterly, local winds are intensified. Mountainous seasides, such as those off Orcas Island, channel winds, deflecting them as much as 90 degrees, and may cause intensified winds where they are forced through a narrow passage or over a saddle between higher hills. For instance, Orcas Island's East Sound often has stronger than average winds during prevailing northerlies.

Fog becomes most common in late July through September, particularly during clear weather when rapid land cooling occurs during the nights. This fog usually clears by early afternoon.

As the Pacific High yields to the Aleutian Low in early fall, prevailing winds shift to southeasterly, and disturbances with gale-force winds become increasingly frequent and intense. The first gales of the season usually occur in late September. By late fall, no weather pattern can be counted on for very long, as a procession of unstable fronts and depressions becomes the rule through the winter. Strong winds are typically southerly throughout the area, but can blow from almost any direction. One particular wintertime hazard is strong northerly winds on clear days, which are a result of outbreaks from arctic high-pressure fronts located in the interiors of Washington or British Columbia. On the other hand, periods of very calm weather also occur during the winter regime, particularly since the low-angle sun has less power to generate local sea breezes. Fog is also possible, especially in January and February, and may persist for several days.

In keeping an eye out for impending weather, there are a few indicators that suggest changes for the worse. Remember that strong winds can develop from very localized circumstances, so the arrival of a bad weather system is not necessary for the onset of trouble.

In general, be most leery of southerly winds, as these suggest the presence of unsettled weather with potential for strong winds. Oncoming wind often can be spotted on the sea in the distance. Rapid shifts in wind direction, particularly counterclockwise changes ("backing" winds, in nautical parlance) to the southeast suggest the arrival of a front. Whatever the wind direction, weather usually arrives from the west, so note the sky in that direction. The development of high clouds or rings around either the sun or moon are harbingers of a front.

By far the most effective predictor is the meteorologist's marine forecast via VHF radio. Continuous-broadcast forecasts and local weather reports are available from four stations, of which at least one can be tuned in anywhere on Washington's inland waters. In the south sound, NOAA's Olympia station broadcasts on WX3 (162.475 MHz) and NOAA's Seattle station broadcasts on WX1 (162.55 MHz). Canadian stations broadcast similar information on WX2 (162.40 MHz) from Victoria or on WX4 (also called Channel 21B, 161.65 MHz) from Vancouver. Most "weather radios" or hand-held VHF transceivers tune at least the first three of these channels. Forecasts are reissued every six hours, with local condition updates every three hours.

Water

Sea temperatures near Seattle vary between fifty-six degrees (Fahrenheit) in August and forty-six degrees in February. A capsize results in hypothermia—body heat loss that can cause death—unless prompt action is taken to get out of the water. Survival time in fifty-degree water can be as little as an hour if you are exerting yourself by swimming (especially when immersing your head), or as much as four hours if you have flotation and are able to hold a heat-retaining fetal position to protect the groin and side areas. Clothing provides some in-the-water insulation (particularly tight weaves and cuffs that trap "dead-water" spaces inside, such as a paddle jacket over other garments). Wet or dry suits can extend survival time indefinitely, but most paddlers in this region find them too hot and uncomfortable to wear except in cold weather.

Hence, well-practiced recovery techniques are especially important in Pacific Northwest waters. Getting out of the water—either back in the boat or ashore—is critical, though the hypothermia may continue due to wind chill.

Early stages of hypothermia include violent shivering, but the individual is lucid and talking clearly and sensibly. Dry clothes and a chance to sit quietly and warm up (either in a warm place or wrapped up to prevent heat loss) are probably the best treatment. Avoid exercise, as that may bring cold blood from the extremities into the body core, lowering the temperature there. This condition, called after drop, may cause serious hypothermia, though the body core could have restored itself to a normal temperature without help. Likewise, do not rub the arms or legs to encourage circulation. Hot drinks also have been known to produce after drop, so they are best avoided unless the condition is clearly a mild one. Likewise, avoid alcohol, which interferes with recovery.

If the person's actions become clumsy, speech becomes slurred, and shivering stops, then the situation is grave and more aggressive treatment is called for. At this point the individual cannot generate enough heat to bring his body temperature back up to normal, and an external heat source is needed. Warm compresses on the torso, neck and head, hot water bottles around these areas inside a sleeping bag, or direct body contact with another person may be required. Use artificial respiration and cardiopulmonary resuscitation (CPR) if necessary.

Marine Traffic Hazards

Some kayakers feel that other boats and ships are as much a danger to paddlers as what nature throws at us. Ships could run down a kayak or upset it in a near miss because they could not see it or because they spot it when too late to avoid it. Pleasure boats could do the same due to inattention at the helm or even coming in for a closer look. Personally, I have never had a close call with either ships or pleasure boats, but marine traffic *is* a hazard that merits attention, particularly in the busier channels of Puget Sound.

Large ships suffer from two disadvantages. First, visibility forward from the ship's bridge is partially obstructed by the hull; from some ships a kayaker is not visible at all when less than one mile ahead! Second, ships cannot maneuver quickly, and emergency actions, like throwing the engines in reverse (which requires some time to accomplish), take time to have an effect and may put the ship out of control. Many ships require more than one mile to stop even with full power astern. Tugs pulling barges are especially unable to change course or to stop quickly.

Consider how small a kayak would appear one mile ahead of a ship's bridge. To get some idea of how visible you are from that ship, imagine your kayak on top of the bridge—probably hardly noticeable— then partially obscure it with whatever waves are around you. The chances that the ship will pick you up on radar are slim. Even if you carried a reflector, it would be too low to the water to produce a significant signal.

So the burden is on you to stay out of a ship's path. As applies to all pleasure craft, you must stay at least one-half mile from approaching ships and one-quarter mile from passing ones. Fortunately, where they are going is usually quite predictable. The major shipping routes in Puget Sound, Rosario Strait, and the Strait of Juan de Fuca have defined traffic lanes, which are marked in red or purple on nautical charts. Some routes are divided into one-way lanes with a separation zone between the two. Ships are supposed to stay within these lanes, so if you can determine where you are in relation to the lane, you can predict where the ship will pass. Though pleasure craft can cross these lanes, they should do so as quickly as possible and otherwise stay out of them. Ships will sometimes deviate from their lane (such as to pass around a sailboat regatta), so be sure to leave some margin for error (for both you and the ship).

Suppose you see a ship coming down a traffic lane that you wish to cross. Should you try to cross ahead of it or wait for it to pass? Obviously, the latter is safest, but circumstances do arise when you find yourself needing to proceed ahead to get clear, or when it seems apparent that you can cross ahead safely (slower tugs with tows are especially tempting). Can you make it?

You need to know something about the ship's speed relative to yours, and your respective distances from your crossing point on the traffic lane. Most ships are much faster than they appear—16 knots is typical in our inland waters, though some freighters may move at their full 20-knot sea speeds. Tugs with tows average 8 knots, with up to 10 knots possible. Assuming 4 knots for your kayak, that means ships may be traveling at four to five times your speed. Make a generous estimate of their speed (using the speeds mentioned) and then compare the ship's distance from where you plan to cross its course to how far you have to go to be clear by one-quarter mile on the other side.

Another way to determine what will happen as you approach a ship on a course perpendicular to your own is to watch the ship's position off your bow as you converge. If the interior angle between your bow and the ship gradually increases, that indicates that you will pass the intersection point first (how much sooner is another question). If it stays constant, you are on a collision course; a decreasing angle indicates you will pass astern.

If you find yourself in a situation in which you fear you cannot get out of a ship's way, emergency signaling with flares or, better yet, with orange smoke, may be your only remedy (though it will probably also bring down upon you the wrath of the Coast Guard, as well as the whole maritime community). The most effective solution is a marine VHF transceiver. Call the ship, let them know what and where you are, and then agree on a solution (do this *before* it is too late for them to take evasive action). Though Channel 16 is the general calling and emergency frequency, ships in Washington's inland waters monitor Channel 14 (Seattle Traffic), or Channel 13 (ships' bridge-to-bridge). If you cannot read the ship's name, call it by position (e.g., "the southbound black container ship off Foulweather Bluff").

For pleasure craft, you will need to rely on visual warnings of your presence, such as a flag attached to a fishing pole if you have a rod holder installed on your deck.

One last hazard is the state ferries. Generally the ferries have much better visibility and maneuverability than ships of comparable size, and they will do their best to go around you. Be especially careful around docked ferries. Be sure that they are not about to leave as you cross ahead (give them a wide berth anyhow), and watch out for their prop wash. Paddling underneath ferry docks is both *illegal* and *dangerous*, as the prop wash from a docking or departing ferry can easily wrap your boat around a piling.

Tides and Currents

In Pacific Northwest waters, staying in tune with tides and tidal currents is as important as keeping an eye on the weather and the marine traffic. Adverse currents can slow or stop your progress, but more important are the hazards of rough water created by currents and possibly made far worse by weather.

Tidal currents (the horizontal movement of water) stem from tides (the vertical movement of water), so paying attention to tide cycles is helpful for picking the safest traveling times.

Tide sizes (the difference between the preceding and following high- or low-tide heights) vary in magnitude during each day, and over longer cycles of weeks and even parts of the year. Current speeds approximate the tide magnitude. For instance, on one ebb tide, there can be a substantial current, but on another the current may be negligible.

Tides in the inland waters of Washington are generally "mixed semidiurnal," which simply means there are two daily cycles of high and low tides, typically one low is considerably lower than the other, as shown in figure 1. The exact shape of the daily curve changes during the month, and at times the smaller cycle may become little more than an afterthought—just a small deviation in the primary cycle.

The strength of currents are roughly proportionate to the size of the ongoing exchange, or the difference between high and low water. Thus, in figure 1, the flood current between lower low (l.l.) water and higher high (h.h.) water will be swifter than that during the exchange from higher low (h.l.) to lower high (l.h.) later in the day. Since the order of this mixed semidiurnal pattern varies from day to day, tide graphs included in some tide tables (*Tidelog* for example, see Useful Publications) are useful for getting an overview of the day's current strengths.

Another important factor to note is the duration of exchanges. Though the average between high tide and low is about six hours, this interval can be as much as nine hours on very big exchanges, or little more than an hour on very small ones (during which there may be hardly any current).

You also should be aware of the bimonthly cycles in tide and current size caused by the alignment of the moon in relation to the earth and the sun. Every fourteen days there is a period of "spring" (from the Saxon word for "active," which has nothing to do with the season) tides

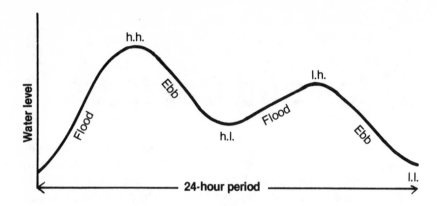

Fig. 1. A typical daily tide cycle in Puget Sound (h.h. = higher high; h.l. = higher low; l.h. = lower high; l.l. = lower low). The differences between highs and lows, and the order in which the higher and lower highs and lows occur, are in constant flux during the month.

and bigger than usual currents when the moon is either full or new (aligned either between or on the far side of the earth in relation to the sun). In between spring tides are periods of "neap" (from the Saxon word for "inactive") tides and currents, which are smaller than average, occurring during quarter moons when the moon is out of alignment with the sun and earth. These cycles exert their biggest influence on outer coast tides and currents. They have less effect on inland tides, though they do affect inland currents to some extent.

More important in Puget Sound and the San Juan Islands is the declination of the moon's orbit from the equator, which follows fifteen-day cyles independently from spring–neap progressions. Similarly, there are two periods of the biggest tides and currents during the year: near the summer and winter solstices in June and December when the sun's declination from the equator is the greatest.

In short, these independent effects can cause dramatic differences in tides and currents, particularly when they coincide. As a consequence, current speeds can be more than twice what they are on another day at the same stage of the tide. So take a close look at your monthly tide tables to keep track of such trends, and note that the two daily cycles follow trends somewhat independent of each other, as each is affected differently by the forces mentioned above. Many tide and current tables include calendars noting these conditions (e.g., full moons and maximum lunar and solar declinations) so that you can see their effects.

Times of no current are called slack water (or in some documents, "minimum flood or ebb current," because the water may not completely stop flowing). The length of the slack is related to the strength of the currents before and after it. *Slack water times do not necessarily coincide with high or low tide.* This difference occurs because the times of the tides can vary from place to place. Tides progress through a region as a very flat but rapidly moving wave, which can be delayed significantly by obstructing landforms like the San Juan Islands. Thus, high and low tide arrive at the south end of the islands about one hour sooner than at the north end.

As a result, during a flooding tide, the water level is higher on the south end of the San Juan Islands than on the north end. The difference, called a hydraulic head, produces a north-flowing current, which continues until the two heights equalize. The slack therefore occurs some time after high tide at the south end and before it on the north end.

The characteristics of the local waterways greatly affect the differences between tides and currents. Hence, mariners use current tables to predict slacks and times of maximum current, and these are far more useful for travel planning than tide tables, though kayakers find the latter useful for timing launches and haul outs.

Predicting Washington Currents

Predictions for Puget Sound and San Juan Islands' currents are found in two types of documents: current tables and current charts or atlases.

Current tables are available from two sources. NOAA's *Current Tables for the Pacific Coast of North America and Asia* is a hefty book that gives current predictions for points between San Diego, California, and the Aleutian Islands and then on to the Philippines. Though the volume is inexpensive, 90 percent of it is worthless if you plan to paddle only the inland waters of Washington. For those who need only local information, the Island Canoe Company has excerpted the NOAA tables into two booklets of currents and tide tables, one for the San Juan Islands and the other for Puget Sound (see Useful Publications). Like the NOAA volume, these are good for one year.

Current tables are composed of two parts, which allow predictions of slack water and maximum currents at specific places. The first part is a calendar of times for slack water and maximum current (with speed predicted for that time) for major reference points. In Washington's inland waters, these are Admiralty Inlet, Tacoma Narrows, Deception Pass, Rosario Strait, and San Juan Channel. Following these are correction factors for many local places, based on the major reference points and showing how local currents will differ from those in time and speed. Table 1 (see Appendix) shows an example of how these local corrections work for a particular day.

The current charts or atlases show schematic pictures of current flows at different stages of the tide. They are easier to use than current tables and are best for getting an overall picture of the flows during a particular time period for route planning. In areas such as the San Juan Islands' east/west channels, where flows are far from intuitively obvious, current charts and atlases can be a great help. Another advantage is that these are perennial rather than annual. However, they are less accurate for predicting slack water times. For places where that is critical, such as Deception Pass, use the current tables.

There are at least three types of current charts and atlases. For Puget Sound, NOAA publishes two sets that are used in conjunction with annual current tables. The Island Canoe Company publishes similar ones that provide some information for predicting differences in velocities based on exchanges, one booklet for Puget Sound and another for the San Juan Islands (see Useful Publications).

For the San Juan Islands, the Canadian Hydrographic Service's *Current Atlas: Juan de Fuca Strait to Strait of Georgia* accurately locates current streams and also the large eddies that occur in this complex area. It also shows how current streams vary in both strength and location depending on size of the tidal exchange. The major difficulty with this book is finding the right chart to use. To do so, you must have a Canadian tide table and make some calculations about the tide times and exchange size. As an alternative, consult my publication, *Washburne's Tables*, published annually by Weatherly Press, which takes you directly to the right chart for any hour of any day without need for tide table, calculations, or daylight saving time corrections.

For Puget Sound, *Tide Prints: Surface Tidal Currents in Puget Sound* by Noel McGary and John W. Lincoln is a similar atlas, though simpler and easier to use. (Unfortunately, it is out of print at this writing.)

Hazards From Currents

The majority of sea kayaking accidents in the Puget Sound area have been caused in part by currents, often aggravated by bad weather. The most widespread dangers are those caused by the interaction of wind and currents.

When wind-generated waves encounter an opposing current (one moving against the wind), the waves are slowed down, or if the current is strong enough, prevented from advancing at all. The waves become steep, much closer together, and may break heavily. The result is a much rougher and more difficult sea for small craft to handle. A channel that has only moderate seas when the current is flowing in the wind's direction may turn into something untenable for kayaks after the current change.

Consequently, kayakers should plan to cross open water at times when the current and wind move in the same direction. Though the wind direction cannot be anticipated with certainty, currents can. (Note that in nautical publications, wind and current directions customarily are expressed in opposite fashion to each other: winds in the direction from which they are *coming*, but currents in the direction toward which they are *going*.)

In November 1983, a kayaker died while crossing from Tumbo Island in British Columbia to Patos Island in the San Juan Islands, a stretch of water known for strong currents. Though the 50-knot winds that caught the party in midchannel could have caused the fatality, the heavy breaking seas were made worse by a large eddy that resulted in currents contrary to the winds during a time when the general flow was in the wind's direction. This eddy could have been identified only with the Canadian *Current Atlas*. (See *Sea Kayaker* magazine, Spring 1984, for a report of the incident.)

In certain situations, waves are forced to break in quite localized areas, called tide rips. Most tide rips occur where land obstructions or underwater shoals impede or change the current flow. They may occur where moving water accelerates because it is being squeezed around a point, through a narrows, or over a shallows (fig. 2). Waves may be able to advance against slower currents up to that place, but cannot get far-

Tide rip near Cypress Island. Waves and the wake from a passing boat are trapped and compressed against an eddy line. The surrounding waters are calm.

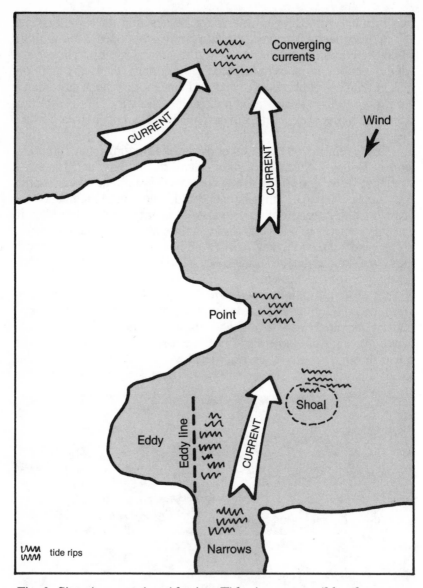

Fig. 2. Situations causing tide rips. Tide rips are possible wherever a current is forced to change speed or direction or where currents converge. Wind is not necessary for rips to form, but generally it makes them much worse.

ther, so they expend their energy in breaking. Hence waves become concentrated and trapped in rips such as at eddy lines (fig. 2), resulting in energy that is released in turbulence.

Sometimes you encounter rips on calm, windless days. Where do the waves come from? They may stem from very low, widely spaced waves that are barely perceptible until they become trapped and intensified in the tide rip area. Also, currents flowing over an irregular bottom may transmit the bottom features to the surface as standing waves (ones that stay in one place), simply another variety of a tide rip.

The rough water in rips also may be created or intensified by the wakes of ships or even pleasure craft. I have seen very minor rips turn into nasty ones after a powerboat passed by. Ship wakes can make such situations far worse.

Where currents intersect, they form an eddy line at their edges. If the difference in current speeds is great enough, waves are unable to cross this barrier, and a rip composed of stalled, multidirectional waves forms adjacent to it (fig. 2). The effect is reminiscent of the clapotis (or intersecting) waves found near a vertical shoreline where waves are being reflected back through the incoming ones. Here the waves become irregular, pyramid shaped, seeming to leap up and disappear unpredictably. Your kayak cannot find an equilibrium on such a rapidly moving surface, so the movement is jerky, you get splashed a lot, and possibly lose balance and capsize.

Occasionally rips are found where there is no apparent reason for their existence. This may result from a large eddy being swept out of the place where it was created and downstream, persisting (with adjacent rips) for quite some time and distance.

It is difficult to predict with certainty where rips will be located even if you know the direction and speed of currents; there is just too little information on charts about bottom features. However, the downstream sides of points or islands (particularly if surrounded by shallows), shoaling areas or underwater reefs, or points where currents intersect (such as where they rejoin after flowing around a large island) are good candidates (see fig. 2). Where the currents are fastest is usually the best tide rip potential. In the San Juan Islands, for instance, colliding currents from Spieden Channel and San Juan Channel regularly form dangerous rips. The particularly fast water at San Juan Channel's south entrance usually has rips, which are at their worst on ebbs against southerly winds.

From a distance, tide rips can be heard as a low roar. Seeing them from the low viewing point of a kayak is harder, particularly on windy days when distant rips are camouflaged by surrounding wind waves. If you find yourself heading for a rip, assess your drift in the current and then try to take evasive action while there is still time. Determining your direction of drift can be done with ranges (sometimes called transits): comparing something in the middle ground (a buoy or a rock) against a feature in the background (a hill or a tree), and observing their movement in relation to each other. Frequent checking of two ranges at right angles to each other (one ahead and one to the side) will help keep track of what the current is doing to you and how effective your paddling is in countering it.

If you cannot avoid the rip, head straight through it. Remember that you are moving with the current, whereas the rip is stationary, and you will soon pass through it. For most rips, there is more noise and splashing than real threat to your stability. I prefer to keep paddling rapidly, each stroke serving as a minibrace to help maintain my equilibrium and direction.

When a current passes along an irregular shoreline or around a point, the flow often breaks off from the main current near shore forming an eddy of still water or even a back eddy—water moving in the opposite direction of the current for a short distance. Such eddies usually form on the downstream side of points, islets, or other obstructions. Sometimes the eddy system will extend out alongside the obstruction as well. Sharply defined eddy lines between the moving water in the current and the still or backward flowing water in the eddy are often accompanied by swirls, turbulence, or even whirlpools. A good example is along the southeast side of Canoe Island in Deception Pass on a strong flood current.

Eddy lines are sometimes responsible for upsetting small craft, including kayaks. The primary cause is inertia; crossing from current to eddy or vice versa involves a rapid transition into water going a different direction, with the boat going sideways through the water and the possibility of capsizing. Consequently, the rule is to lean and brace *downstream*, or to put it another way, to present your bottom to the current. Also, the tremendous turbulence and up- and down-welling water possible in eddy lines can cause strong torquing forces on a kayak's hull, possibly causing you to capsize.

Crossing powerful eddy lines is best done quickly and at right angles. (Crossing through weaker eddy lines will be discussed later.) Keep paddling at a rapid pace so that strokes can serve as braces.

Using Eddies to Go Upstream

Usually, wherever currents are found, there also are eddies along the shore made up of either still water or localized currents moving upstream for some distance. The more irregular the shoreline, the more extensive the eddy system. A good example is San Juan Island's shore along Spieden Channel. During one strong spring tide ebb, I and a group of young campers in canoes easily traversed this shoreline via its eddy system, while in midchannel, two sailboats going the same way stood stationary under both sail and power. We had long since rounded Limestone Point and gone our separate ways before the sailors pulled themselves out of the current's grasp.

Generally, eddies form on the downstream side of points of land, or in indentations along the shoreline. The boundaries between the main current stream and the eddy may be marked by turbulence or changes in the texture of the water's surface. They may be difficult to see in slower currents. Within the eddy itself, which may cover an extensive area, water can move in many different directions. Most eddies are actually circling water, though the patterns vary. Some water may move slowly downstream, while nearby, the flow is upstream—a back eddy. I usually move around as I progress through eddies to find the most favorable currents, using cues such as the direction in which the kelp lies.

More than likely, you will be forced to paddle hard to progress from one eddy upstream to the next, usually rounding a point where, for a short distance, the current sweeps along the shore as fast as in midstream. Such "eddy hopping" requires some positioning, careful boat handling, and perhaps a burst of everything you have for a short, hard pull. Use the still water usually found just downstream from the point to build up some speed and inertia, then break out into the opposing current as far upstream and close to the point as possible. Head as directly upstream as possible as you enter the main current; otherwise the boat's bow will be pushed out and you will find yourself heading perpendicular to where you intended to go, rapidly losing ground. If this occurs, rather than trying to recover, just continue to turn downstream and reenter the eddy you just left and try again.

Going Ashore

Kayakers are amphibious creatures, at home on both sea and land, and crossing between them far more easily and frequently than other boaters. In many other parts of the country, going ashore often puts you in somebody's front yard or private preserve. By contrast, Washington is well endowed with public lands hospitable to boaters. Because these are managed by a variety of different agencies, each with its own purposes and policies, it is helpful for kayakers to know in advance who is in charge of what place, and how that affects what can be expected there.

Also, many of the trips listed in this book are two days long or more, so you will need some camping gear and skills. This book offers no primer on the latter, but calls attention to a few peculiarities of kayak camping along Washington's inland waters. Among those are things that kayakers can do to minimize their effects on these wildlands and their wildlife while ashore or paddling nearby.

Public Lands

Most public lands are available for use by everyone, but some (particularly national wildlife refuges) are not. Following is a brief description of the different jurisdictions and what kayakers can expect in each.

NATIONAL PARKS. There is one national park on Washington's inland shoreline: San Juan Island National Historic Park, commemorating the 1859 so-called Pig War between Britain and the United States. There are two units, both on San Juan Island: American Camp at the southern end and English Camp on the northeast side. These include historical reconstructions and interpretative programs and facilities for picnicking but not for camping. (The National Park Service avoids providing camping facilities where neighboring agencies can do it, as is the case in the San Juan Islands.) Camping is not allowed on the park's undeveloped lands.

NATIONAL WILDLIFE REFUGES. Nisqually National Wildlife Refuge and San Juan Islands National Wildlife Refuge are the two federal refuges in the area described in this book. The Nisqually refuge

Cypress Head, a DNR recreation site on Cypress Island.

allows boating in the delta and walking onshore as long as nesting sites are not disturbed. The San Juan Islands refuge includes almost all of the small islets, rocks, and reefs in that area, and some larger islands such as Flattop, Skipjack, and Smith islands. Many of these are also part of the National Wilderness Preservation System. No landings are allowed on any of these eighty-odd places without permission from the U.S. Fish and Wildlife Service, which requests that you stay at least two hundred yards from these refuge islands. Such islands are particularly inviting to kayakers, but this is a case of protecting birds' and seals' rights to peaceful nesting and haul outs, and the U.S. Fish and Wildlife Service will not compromise these goals to provide public recreation. Where units of the refuge are encountered on routes in this book, they will be mentioned as a caution to keep off of them. They are usually well marked with signs to that effect. Two islands in the refuge, Matia Island and Turn Island, have portions leased to Washington State Parks. You may camp in these park areas and walk the trails on the rest of the islands or land on most of the beaches as long as birds' nesting sites are not nearby.

WASHINGTON STATE PARKS. State parks provide the most extensive opportunities for both day use and camping throughout Washington's inland waterways. Though most of Washington's park sites are developed, some of the marine (boat access only) parks are totally undeveloped—particularly small islands, such as Victim Island in West Sound—and overnight camping is not permitted. With a few exceptions, camping is allowed at the many small island parks where sanitation (a pit toilet) is provided. Most of these also have picnic tables and fire rings, but no drinking water. Examples of such undeveloped camping sites are Blind Island, McMicken Island, and Posey Island state parks. There is no camping fee, largely because it is too much trouble to collect it.

Aside from these small islands, most marine state parks charge a fee of $3.00 per campsite, which is collected through self-registration stations. These fees usually are not in effect between October and April, though the schedule varies from park to park. Technically, park rangers could also charge kayaks a fee of $3.50 for mooring, even if they were hauled up on the beach overnight rather than tied to the dock. The vast majority will not levy this, but one ranger told me that a few parks do.

A few state parks with more highly developed campgrounds for autos and recreational vehicles also are popular with kayakers. The fee for these sites is $6.00, but most of these parks also have at least a few less developed sites near the water for boaters at a $3.00 fee (consult the ranger). Examples are Jarrell Cove and Spencer Spit state parks.

Dispersed camping (that is, establishing your own campsite in the woods) is not permitted in any of Washington's state parks. This is to prevent the impact that camping has on wildlands from spreading. It is also to avoid conflicts with other management goals such as eagle habitat management in the San Juan Islands.

Be prepared to take your trash home with you. Many marine state parks now have a pack-it-out garbage program to combat the high cost of removing the mountains of trash deposited by boaters on the island parks.

DEPARTMENT OF NATURAL RESOURCES (DNR) RECREATION AREAS. The Department of Natural Resources manages some of the best-kept secrets along Washington shorelines. The DNR's recreation areas are picnic and camp areas that provide most of the same facilities that state parks provide, but without a fee for their use. Facilities are simple (pit toilets, usually no water), and maintenance is infrequent, as DNR covers a large area with a tiny staff. (Ironically, as of this writing, DNR still provides and empties trash cans at every site I have visited.)

One of the least-known public wildlands is DNR "school lands." These usually undeveloped parcels are managed to provide income (usually from timber) for local schools, and hence the name. The DNR has no objection to public recreation, even camping, as long as fires are not built. These parcels can be identified on DNR maps (see Useful

Squaxin Island State Park.

Publications).

The DNR also manages the state's public tidelands, which are scattered throughout Puget Sound and the San Juan Islands (more than half of the tidelands in the latter are public). These are rarely identified by signs, but booklets and maps showing their locations are available from DNR (see Useful Publications). Almost all of the public tidelands extend only as high as the mean high tide line unless the uplands are publicly owned too. Hence, I do not feel these are very useful for kayakers except for a quick leg stretch or some clam digging. Remember that you will be trespassing if you wander above the high tide line.

Camping

WATER. To be surrounded by water without a drop to drink is the seafarer's dilemma also shared by sea kayakers unfamiliar with camping in Washington's inland waters. The great majority of campsites along these shores have no drinking water, and some (Jones Island State Park, for example) often run out of it midway through the summer. Many of those that do have a water system shut it off between fall and spring.

Unless you are going somewhere where you know there will be water, carry your own. Take along enough to tide you over should you have to stay longer because of bad weather (instead of being forced to beg water from yachts or head for home in dangerous conditions).

Three quarts per person per day usually is enough if you are careful with it. Wash dishes in salt water (followed by a sparing rinse with fresh water to prevent corrosion) and add it to fresh water for cooking. A half-and-half combination is about right for water that will be poured off (such as for boiling noodles), and one part salt water to two or more parts fresh water is a good ratio when the water stays in the food (such as in cooking rice).

A collapsible two- to three-gallon jug fits well in most kayaks. A larger number of smaller water bottles, however, are easier to fit in a small boat, provide better trim, and give better protection against water leaking away.

FIRES AND STOVES. Though most public campsites have fire rings or grates, firewood is not always available. In most places, driftwood is the only option, and during the busy months all the smaller pieces have been collected. Bring a saw and a hatchet or an ax. I prefer to carry a backpacking stove to do my cooking, and I build a fire only for warmth or the aesthetic value.

Beach fires generally are not allowed, both because of the unsightly scars they leave, and because they can get out of control and spread to the uplands. Wildfires are a particular fear in drier places such as the San Juan Islands during the summer, so build fires only in designated rings and never leave them unattended.

For comfortable camping during the off-season, I find a larger tent heated with a small wood stove makes the difference between tolerable existence and real pleasure. My winter shelters are floorless nylon wall tents; one I made for myself, and the other is a commercial model that I modified by adding a hole and pocket for the stovepipe flange in the end wall. A woven polypropylene tarp covers the floor away from the stove.

Wood stoves small enough to fit in a kayak are available commercially (both folding or rigid models). I make my own out of one and one-half- to two-gallon gas cans or from sheet metal; these will fit behind my seat in the kayak and last about one season. The flue consists of two sections of either two-inch galvanized (not aluminum) gutter downspout, or three-inch stovepipe. The two pipe elbows store inside the stove. Setting the stove up on a few rocks leaves almost no trace from its heat after the tent is removed.

RACCOONS. Cuteness is the sole virtue of the ubiquitous raccoon (*Larcenus pestiferens*). You can expect a visit from these bold and persistent critters at any time, day or night. Their ability to cart off large food packages is notorious. I once awoke to find that a twenty-pound duffel bag full of food had been dragged 150 feet during the night.

James Island State Park is home to the commando elite of raccoons, well-known for their bravado and larcenous skills, which they continuously hone on park visitors. The tenacity and deviousness of this cadre is unequaled in all the San Juan Islands. They never slack from their mission and apparently never sleep. Neither will you. I recall one winter's night when their persistent efforts to liberate my food from my tent (where I lay clutching it) reduced me to chasing them through the bushes in my underwear with a flashlight, dementedly determined to drive them all into the sea. (Sorry, I failed.)

Hanging food is protection only if done cleverly enough to foil these excellent climbers. Another solution is to store food in the large plastic jars in which Greek olives are shipped. Reportedly raccoon proof, these jars have large screw lids, and one will hold several days' worth of food. You usually can buy them at Greek restaurants and delicatessens.

A final note to aid a half-decent night's sleep: bring everything that clanks or rattles (cookware, etc.) into the tent with you, or suffer listening to the raccoons examining it all night.

SOLITUDE. An important ingredient to satisfactory camping, solitude may be the most difficult to find during the summer months and particularly on major holidays. I spent one Memorial Day weekend sleeping on the beach at Sucia Island, where all campsites were occupied. During such peak times, try to aim for places less attractive to overnight boaters: sites without docks, moorings, or protected anchorages. Look to some of the lesser-known DNR sites, especially those without overland access and poor landings for boats.

One major impact on camp solitude are the canoeing and kayaking groups from YMCA Camp Orkila (pronounced Orc-*eye*-la) on Orcas Island. There may be as many as five of these groups of a dozen or so youngsters on the water and camping throughout the San Juan Islands at any one time. Fortunately, they do have a fixed schedule of campsites, so you can arrange your trip to avoid them by calling the camp (382-5009 in Seattle or 1-(206)-376-2678 on Orcas Island).

Minimum Impact

Though it would be beyond the scope of this book to present a primer on low-impact camping skills, there are a few situations relating to the sea kayaker in this area that merit attention. Though the effect of each person is low, there are now enough of us that some problem patterns are emerging and will increase with kayaking's popularity unless each of us is aware of our effect on the environment.

Though kayakers are probably the least likely boaters to disrupt wildlife, they do affect them, nonetheless, to the point that it concerns wildlife managers. Marine mammals (particularly seals) and birds are most vulnerable when they are bearing and rearing their young. Mother seals may abandon their pups if they become separated from them or if the pups are handled by humans. Seal pups do not know enough to fear humans, and there have even been reports of pups trying to climb aboard kayaks! Stay clear of mothers with young and paddle away from pups if they approach you.

Birds are particularly sensitive when they are incubating their eggs. (The incubation period varies from species to species.) Bald eagles are a special concern to wildlife managers, as they may abandon eggs if there is too much human activity in the vicinity of the nest (a major reason that camping is either prohibited or confined to one area in popular eagle-nesting areas such as Patos Island). Eagles are incubating between late March and May, so be especially unobtrusive on shore or while paddling along shore in eagle country at that time.

Another problem is independent camping in nondesignated sites. One state park ranger told me: "Sea kayakers used to be my favorite user group, but now they're becoming a problem group. Too many of them like to find their own campsite in the woods, and even though they are careful about fires and what they leave behind, they tell their friends about it, and soon I've got another well-established illegal campsite."

The problem is that Washington's coastline is simply too popular to provide the wilderness-style camping that many kayakers seek. For that, you simply must head north into British Columbia or find it in the mountains without your kayak. There are opportunities for legal independent camping on undeveloped DNR school lands, but these are rare and often not very attractive. (Do not build fires if you do camp on these lands.)

We kayakers can cultivate our own interests by assuring that we are the most inexpensive and inoffensive user group for park managers to provide for. Support the pack-it-out garbage programs and avoid using the garbage cans that are provided if you can take it home. Stick to designated campsites, and when in doubt, ask.

Going Paddling

In this chapter I discuss information you need to consider when preparing for a kayak outing. For instance, how can you evaluate whether your condition and skills are appropriate for the trip you have in mind, and whether the distances are appropriate for the time you have as well as the amount of energy you are willing to put out. Additionally, where will you park your car and launch your boat. I also will discuss a little-known but very handy way for kayakers to ride the Washington State ferries, with boats and gear as carry-ons. Finally, I will examine the pleasures and perils of paddling during the off-season in these inland waters.

Trip Planning

NAUTICAL CHARTS. Charts for Washington's inland waters are issued by NOAA and sold by many nautical supply retailers or kayak shops around the region. Which charts cover any particular area is shown in "Nautical Chart Catalog 2: United States, Pacific Coast," a free brochure available where the charts are sold.

Two and sometimes three chart alternatives, with different scales of coverage, are available for any locality in this area. The least expensive coverage is 1:80,000 charts, available in large, single sheets or folios containing three sheets printed on lighter paper. The folios are called Small Craft (SC) charts, and two of them (18423 SC and 18445 SC) will cover all the waters discussed in this book. The detail at this scale is adequate for cruising, and the light paper and small pages are easy to fold into a chart case.

Larger-scale charts give you a more intimate and detailed view of the shorelines, but increase your costs for coverage and result in more frequent turning and refolding charts in your chart case. Though I prefer scales of 1:40,000 or larger for the wilder shores of British Columbia and Alaska to spot good landing sites, I find the 1:80,000 barely adequate but serviceable in Washington. In Washington land ownership is more relevant to getting ashore than shoreline composition and foreshore extent (the area between high and low tide, which shows how far you might have to carry your boat if the tide is out).

Loading up the boats at Jones Island.

DAILY DISTANCE. The distance you cover on a daily basis depends on how much time you are willing to spend in the boat. This factor is far more important than your paddling strength or the boat's speed. In general, most people cruise at between 3 and 4 knots (nautical miles per hour). With stops to look around, rest, or stretch my legs, I average about 2 knots for the day as a whole (time between getting under way in the morning and hauling out for the evening divided by miles traveled). I think that 10 nautical miles per day is a comfortable distance for most people in average paddling conditions (barring strong head winds). Using the currents can make a dramatic difference. A group of us once clocked ourselves at 5 knots over a ten-mile distance of fairly leisurely paddling with a favorable current.

WEATHER ALLOWANCES AND ALTERNATIVE ROUTES. One of the most dangerous situations into which kayakers get themselves is *having* to be home at a certain time. This self-induced pressure prompts them to paddle during unsettled weather in exposed places. Some trip locations are less dangerous than others. For instance, paddling two miles along a shoreline against gusting 20-knot winds is far safer than paddling a two-mile crossing under the same conditions. Some places have route options, which offer safer but longer ways back to your launch point or to somewhere from which you could hitch a ride back to your car. I have tried to incorporate the existence of such options in the trip ratings for this book.

The more exposed the route and the fewer route options there are, the more time should be allowed for bad weather contingencies. How much depends on the time of year and the regional weather pattern at the time. A large, stable high-pressure area over the Northwest in July probably indicates the least likelihood of being weather-bound. In January, however, weather patterns are usually too changeable to count on forecasted conditions for even a day in advance. During the summer months, you may want to consider the forecast for the period you will be paddling and choose a trip rating accordingly. During the off-season, periods of bad weather should be assumed. Either build extra time into the itinerary or choose less exposed trips. (Because of the increased hazard potential during the off-season, all trip ratings in this book should be considered as one rating more hazardous during that time.)

Choosing a Trip

New sea kayakers have difficulty identifying trips where the conditions are within their paddling limits. Saltwater trips are more difficult to classify than those on rivers where conditions can be predicted quite accurately. Almost any saltwater trip can be mirror smooth on the best of days, and a raging sea in the worst of conditions. There is no sure way to avoid the latter. Overconfidence comes easily on those glassy days, and many sea kayakers have gotten more than what they bargained for by taking on more challenging routes after better-than-average weather on early trips. It is wise to start out slowly and to experience a range of weather conditions in protected situations before testing your skills in more exposed places.

Trip Ratings

I have rated trips based primarily on the potential for trouble from either weather or currents and the availability of escape routes. These ratings take into account the amount of protection provided by land to prevent seas from building in windy conditions, and the distance from shore that paddling each route requires. The ratings also consider current speeds and the hazards they can introduce, and hazards from marine shipping traffic. Daily paddling distances may be longer for trips with a more challenging rating as determined by either a minimum loop distance or the least distance between campsites.

Even the lowest rating presumes some kayak experience—*no* saltwater trip is recommended for your first time in a kayak. A first-time kayaker should start by learning basic boat-handling skills in a pool and then in lake water (which is likely to be warmer and smoother than the inland seas).

These ratings are effective late spring through early fall. *Each trip moves up one rating during the off-season*, October through April (see Paddling During the Off-season, p. 48).

A trip designated as **protected** is suitable for novice kayakers possessing basic boat-handling skills and rudimentary familiarity with nautical charts. Daily distances are seven miles or less. Routes mostly follow the shore, with no crossings of over one-half mile. Waters are largely protected by nearby landforms, and sea currents never exceed .5 knot. Tide rips are unlikely.

A trip designated as **moderate** is suitable for kayakers who have well-established boat-handling skills, who have had some previous saltwater paddling experience, are aware of current and weather patterns, and can use current and weather prediction resources for planning. Daily distances may be up to ten miles on waters where crossings up to one mile are required, and wind and current could cause dangerous seas. Marine shipping lanes may need to be crossed. Currents may attain 1.5 knots for short distances and tide rips are possible in opposing wind conditions. **Moderate** + indicates the presence of a localized hazard that can be avoided by timing your travel or by choosing an alternative route.

A trip designated as **exposed** is suitable for experienced sea kayakers who have a thorough understanding of weather and currents and their interaction, and who can handle their boats in rough water. Major marine shipping lanes may need to be crossed. Daily distances may be ten miles or more, with travel in exposed seas one mile or more from shore. Currents may attain more than 2 knots, and tide rips are likely. Trips in this class become very risky during the off-season and should be undertaken only with ample buffer time to await safe weather.

A trip designated as **deadly** is suitable only for heroic characters or armchair expeditionaries for whom life or talk, respectively, is cheap. Kayakers must have a metaphysical relationship with their boats, relish discomfort, and revel in acclaim. Rogue waves and great, sucking whirlpools are common. Marine traffic is hostile and will ram if possible. Trips of this high caliber are rare in Washington's inland waters, and are not represented in this book.

Kayaks and Washington State Ferries

The Washington State ferry system enriches the already extensive paddling possibilities in Puget Sound and the San Juan Islands. At present, carry-on kayaks are treated as luggage, and you pay only for yourself as a foot passenger. Washington State ferry officials have assured me that foot passsengers will be allowed to continue carrying kayaks aboard although, eventually, there is likely to be a fee for those kayaks (as there is for bicycles). But at this writing, the ferry system has no plans for introducing such a fee.

The cost savings for carrying a kayak on board (as opposed to driving) are greatest for one person alone. The savings decrease with the size of the party (assuming that all persons and boats use one vehicle when driving). For instance, a foot passenger pays $4.35 for a round trip from Anacortes into the San Juan Islands (1985 summer rates). A round trip to the islands with a car would cost that person $15.55. Two people driving with their boats on one vehicle would each pay $9.90 for the round trip. When the ferries do add a kayak charge, it probably still will be cheaper for a single paddler or a couple to carry on their kayaks though using a car may prove more cost effective for larger groups.

The cost savings is not as significant as the flexibility that carrying a kayak on board allows in choosing paddling routes. For instance, many kayakers leave their vehicles in Anacortes, walk onto the ferry with their kayaks, ride to one of the islands, paddle to any of several other islands, and then catch a ferry back to Anacortes. (As an alternative, kayakers can paddle all the way back to Anacortes—but the one-way ferry fare is

Foot passengers may carry kayaks on Washington State ferries at no additional charge.

the same as a round-trip fare.) It also enables fine day excursions such as paddling from Winslow to Bremerton using the Seattle–Winslow ferry and the Bremerton–Seattle ferry to start and finish. (See my book *The Coastal Kayaker: Kayak Camping on the Alaska and B.C. Coast*, p. 154, for a description of this route.) Carrying a kayak on board also provides a significant bad weather fallback, particularly in the San Juan Islands, where paddling to a nearer or less exposed terminal may be safer than paddling back to your car, wherever it is parked.

During the summer months, large numbers of foot passengers with kayaks make the San Juan Islands ferry run particularly hectic. The staff at the Anacortes ferry terminal recommends a few things to make it easier for everyone.

First, arrive at least one hour early. This will give you time to find parking and to get your boat and gear ready to board. You are welcome to use the long-term parking lot, but you may have to go one or more miles up the highway to park if it is full.

The biggest problem that carry-on kayaks pose for the ferry staff is the multiple trips that kayakers make to get their gear aboard, which delays loading cars. They ask that you consolidate as much as possible and/or use a boat cart to minimize the trips.

Presently, kayaks are assured of boarding the next ferry, regardless of the backlog of cars waiting, some of which may have to take an even later ferry. (This may be a significant advantage on a busy summer weekend.) At this writing there are no plans to limit the number of kayaks per ferry, though it may come to that if the number of carry-ons continues to increase. The ferry staff asks that groups with five or more kayaks call the Anacortes ferry terminal in advance so that a vehicle space on the ferry can be reserved for them. Telephone 1-(206)-293-8166 and ask for the agent.

Kayakers who carry on their boats need a put-in within walking distance of the ferry terminal where they disembark. In almost all cases, there is someplace to do that, though some locations are a fair distance away, and at some, there may be a fee for the privilege. These are described in table 2 (see Appendix) and also are discussed under trips that involve those ferry terminals.

Launching and Parking

Finding a place to launch your kayak and leave your car while you are gone can be something of a problem. Some areas along Washington's inland shorelines are well endowed with public facilities providing both access to the water and convenient parking. Other areas, particularly in certain parts of the San Juan Islands, are limited in public shore access or parking areas, or both. Orcas Island has the least public access and parking, and private property is the probable option—at a cost.

In researching this book, I encountered bad feelings about kayakers among Orcas Island residents. Their sentiments have nothing to do with kayakers on the water, but with kayakers getting to the water. One waterfront resident reported finding two kayakers sorting out gear on her lawn in preparation for launching. A marina owner found five kayakers loading their boats on his float, preempting spaces for boats stopping to shop in his store. Another islander summed up her feelings this way: "I identify with kayakers and why they come here and know they appreciate the same things about the islands that I do. But some of them act like they think the whole place is a park, where they have a right to everything at no cost to themselves. They take, but give nothing back; they rarely buy anything in the stores like the other boaters do. When they expect to use our property too, that's the last straw!"

Such bad feelings are certainly not in kayakers' best interests, particularly since it is the nature of our means of travel to interact more with people along the way than most other boaters do. The situation is easily redressed when attention is paid to both our actions and attitudes.

First, we should overcome our reluctance to buy locally, even if prices are a bit higher. If possible, buy food locally. Expect to pay for launching or parking privileges on private land. (For each of the trips in this book originating on Orcas Island, I have listed private launching/ parking sites and the fees as well as what public ones exist.) Most important, *ask* before using any private land, even if there are not any "No Trespassing" signs, and even if you have a good reason (one more substantial than just for convenience) in the first place. (Imagine how you would feel if you were approached every weekend by people wanting to use your beach.)

On Shaw Island, there have been conflicts with the Franciscan nuns who operate the ferry dock and the adjoining general store. The nuns complain that kayakers have snarled vehicle traffic at the landing and use their floats east of the ferry dock for launching. Until recently, they contested kayakers' access to the beach just west of the landing, which has since been determined to be a public right-of-way. This is a fine launch point for carry-on kayaks, but avoid parking a car there. Get your boats and gear down to the beach as quickly as possible to avoid congestion of the area near the store (which carries all sorts of provisions appealing to kayakers).

Finally, before we leave this downbeat topic, I strongly suggest that you avoid Waldron Island entirely in your San Juan Islands travels. There have been enough unfortunate incidents there involving kayakers to prompt the residents' council to formally protest to the state for attracting boating use to the island through the DNR's tideland publications. Be advised that, other than public tidelands, there are no public beaches, toilets, or parklands, and that you are *not* welcome to visit there. Please paddle elsewhere.

Paddling During the Off-season

For me, paddling in Washington's inland waters during the off-season is just as appealing as during the summer. In fact, there is much about it that I prefer.

During the winter months, there are fewer boats with which to share the waterways. A quiet wildness comes from the scarcity of boats, and from having whole marine park islands to yourself as you would never expect in your wildest dreams of summer. Other boaters met are kindred spirits who appreciate the advantages of winter boating to the extent that they are foolish enough to be out there, too. Boaters are more inclined to say a few words as they pass one another, acknowledging some sort of bond.

Then there are the many seabird species, which are rarely seen in the warmer months. There are the overcast November days, when the air and the sea are languid, almost paralyzed, from dawn to dusk, which rarely happens in summer. Silence is broken only by the distant conversations of rafts of floating seabirds or the gentle breathing of a passing harbor porpoise.

The question of imminent weather is seldom far from the winter paddler's mind, and seemingly never so far from his or her ability to predict it. Winter in Puget Sound is a stern, no-nonsense time of year. Things get done on nature's terms, or suffer the consequences.

The changeability and strength of the winds during the winter months are doubtlessly major hazards to contend with. I feel that upgrading the trips to a more severe rating for the off-season is entirely justified for this reason.

Weather is simply more unpredictable during the off-season. Fronts and low-pressure systems follow each other in much closer succession. You must expect more from what comes than you do during the more benign and settled summer months. And you must paddle in rougher and more uncertain conditions than you might prefer. As you move along, there is the pressure of time; twilight lurks never far away. With the stronger winds and the more fully developed seas, tide rips can occur where they rarely do in less windy times of the year. And, what is lacking is that admittedly reassuring audience of passing pleasure craft that, during the summer, is eagerly watching for the chance to rescue you. They are all snug in their moorings, while winter wilderness is all yours.

I recall one trip from Lopez Island to James Island through Thatcher Pass on an unsettled November day. It bore little resemblance to the placid summer "pond" across which I had lazed my way countless times before. Winds gusted from one direction, settled to flat calm, shifted, and blew hard out of another direction in the space of an hour. Rips popped up where I had never seen them before. The daylight faded far too soon, and through it all, there was nary another boat to be seen.

Other memorable moments of kayak terror have taken place in the winter. The seas may not have been significantly bigger than those of the summer, but there was frequently the fear of a medium sea about to become a nasty one. Then, the chill of the splashes on my hands and face and how distant the shore suddenly seemed became all the more apparent.

You will notice other differences in the winter. Beaches, particularly gravel ones, become steeper. The characteristically bigger waves tend to move the beach material more, piling it up at the current water level so that there is a definite berm or steep drop-off. The results are two. First, launching or landing may result in a raised bow on the beach and the stern in the water, a precarious position that often results in a spill. Second, a "dumping" surf, one that abruptly spills its energy close to shore, may hinder entering or exiting the boat.

One January morning a friend and I launched at Clark Island into a heavy chop coming across Rosario Strait. Because of the surf on the beach, we each buttoned up in our boats before launching and paddle poling ourselves off the steep, slippery beach. I slithered out with no problem, but the sharp stern of my friend's Mariner buried itself in the steep berm, leaving him teetering precariously in the surf until he could lever himself off with his paddle.

Daily wind patterns from summer no longer hold, particularly the axiom of least wind in early morning. These summer cycles are largely generated by the heating of land masses and consequent convection currents. But the low angle of the sun in the winter gives it far less heating power, and the land often remains as cold or colder than the sea, generating little convection.

Next to weather, the biggest constraint on paddling during the off-season is the short daylight, which seems to impinge on kayak travel even more than other forms of self-propelled recreation. The main factor is the relatively long time that kayakers need between getting up in the morning and getting under way. In comparing notes with others, I find that two hours is about the standard between crawling out of the tent and paddling away.

Hence, during the shortest days of the year, trying to make ten miles a day requires using every minute of daylight. If you hate rising before dawn as I do, and it gets light at 8:00 A.M., that means getting on the water at 10:00 A.M. Assuming about 2 knots for travel speed including breaks and a brief lunch stop, you should be reaching the next camp at about 3:00 P.M., with an hour of fading light left in which to get ashore and set up camp. I am particularly wary of being caught on the water at dusk in the winter, since a quick change of weather (for the worse) in the dark is especially unnerving and dangerous.

Camping likewise requires the acceptance of some austerities in return for your own private reserve of gorgeous winter wildlands, perhaps bartering an evening under cover in a continuous downpour for the frosty morning's walk along a marine park pathway that shows no recent footprints. And for me, the challenge of trying to set up a warm and comfortable evening's nest in spite of what is going on outside is a large part of the season's appeal.

Clothing for the off-season should be able to shed water and wind. With the heavier precipitation and stronger winds, you will want to wear a paddle jacket most of the time. A good barrier against the substantially greater wind-chill factor (even in light breezes) is important for your safety as well as comfort. Some paddlers wear dry suits, though they find them too warm for summer paddling. A glove that guards against both wetness and cold air is also important. So far I have found pogies to be the most effective protection without cramping paddling style.

Places to Go—
The San Juan Islands

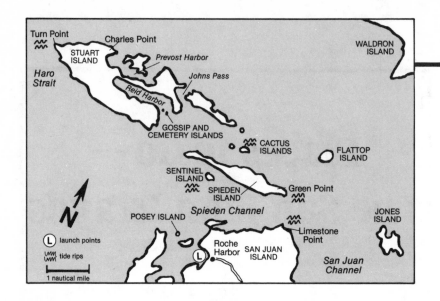

Stuart Island

I consider Stuart Island to be among the "wildest" of the San Juan Island trips, both because part of this area is dramatically natural but also because the tidal forces are at their strongest here. This is no place for novices. You are likely to generate some excitement just paddling to and from Stuart Island, but its shorelines and two park areas are sure to make the visit a pleasure.

DURATION: Two days or more; three days recommended.

RATING: Exposed.

CHARTS AND OTHER NAVIGATION AIDS: NOAA charts 18423 SC, 18421 (both 1:80,000) or 18432 (1:25,000), and San Juan Islands current tables. The Canadian Hydrographic Service's *Current Atlas: Juan de Fuca Strait to Strait of Georgia* is very helpful for route planning.

PLANNING CONSIDERATIONS: Currents in this area are very strong, and powerful rips form in all weather conditions. Coordination with currents is *essential* for both efficient travel and safety, particularly when there are larger than average tides.

Getting There and Launching

To reach the San Juan Islands, exit Interstate 5 at Burlington and follow Highway 20 west to Anacortes. Continue approximately four miles, following signs to the San Juan Islands ferry terminal. To reach Roche Harbor on San Juan Island, drive from the Friday Harbor ferry landing straight ahead two blocks to Second Street South, and turn right. After three blocks bear left on Guard Street, then right on Tucker Avenue. At the fork, bear left onto Roche Harbor Road. The total distance is approximately ten miles.

Launching at Roche Harbor on San Juan Island is allowed without charge at the resort's ramp or the adjoining grassy area about one hundred yards south of the resort. (The staff at Hotel de Haro maintains that there is no fee for this, but kayakers report they have been charged to launch there.) Parking is in a pay lot across the street at $2.00 per car per day.

Alternative launch points include Friday Harbor on San Juan

Turn Point State Park on Stuart Island.

Island, Orcas Island, or Shaw Island.

To launch from Friday Harbor, use the public dock east of the ferry landing. Overnight parking is very limited and almost unobtainable in Friday Harbor during the summer (check in the port office at the public dock for possibilities).

To launch from Orcas Island or Shaw Island, see the Central San Juan Islands chapter for instructions.

Routes

ROCHE HARBOR, SAN JUAN ISLAND TO STUART ISLAND:
Exposed. The round-trip paddling distance is ten miles. This is the shortest, least hazardous, and most popular approach to Stuart Island. Add ten miles if launching from Friday Harbor.

Paddling between San Juan Island and Stuart Island probably requires more careful timing with the currents than anywhere else in the San Juan Islands. Though the crossings are generally a mile or less, the strong currents that run through these channels and the associated tide rips earn this trip its **exposed** rating. However, since tidal cycles are predictable, careful planning and timing can make this a safer trip than one with the same rating due to longer crossings and associated bad-weather exposure.

The primary hazards occur in Spieden Channel. At the eastern end, between Green Point on Spieden Island and Limestone Point on San Juan Island, is some of the fastest water in the San Juan Islands; it runs over 5 knots on the year's biggest spring tides. Most significant are two powerful and extensive tide rips that form off of both points on either set of the tide. The rip off Limestone Point forms one hundred yards or more offshore, but the Green Point rip extends in quite close to Spieden Island's shoreline. There are less severe rips at the western end of the channel in the vicinity of Danger Shoal, Center Reef, and Sentinel Island.

The channels north of Spieden Island, on either side of the Cactus Islands, also run very swiftly, though you will find no local reference stations for them in the current tables. Currents here and in the northern San Juan Channel are somewhat fickle, particularly after the tide changes when patterns of flow around each side of San Juan Island are not yet established. One kayaker bound for Jones Island from Flattop Island reported being carried to Spieden Island on the flood current, when it should have been flowing in the opposite direction.

Since the total distance from San Juan Island to Stuart Island is too far to paddle in any slack current period, give most priority to Spieden Channel, and then round Spieden Island in whichever direction is most convenient (keeping in mind the possible rips close to Green Point). Currents in Spieden Channel are slower between Davison Head and Sentinel Island than farther to the east. This area might be a good place to start at the tail end of the flood tide, then ride the ebb current west along Spieden Island, and finally take advantage of that current to reach Reid Harbor, compensating to the northeast against its flow.

Most of the small islands and rocks north of Spieden Island are units of the San Juan Islands National Wildlife Refuge; *do not approach them.*

If you make a late start from Roche Harbor or run late on the return, tiny Posey Island State Park outside the harbor's two approaches makes a suitable overnight spot. As on other small islands in Washington's park system, there is one outhouse but no water. Three campsites are located on the south, east, and west sides, with wind protection from the trees and brush at the center depending on wind direction. Since Posey Island is close to Roche Harbor's many summer homes, you can expect company in the summer months from young party makers who bring their music with them.

For camping at Stuart Island, either Reid or Prevost harbors are suitable for kayakers. Both are part of Stuart Island State Park. It is one of the few marine parks in the San Juan Islands where you can count on finding fresh water; the well rarely runs dry. The fee for camping is $3.00 levied through a self-registration station.

Reid Harbor is my favorite for camping, particularly the sites on either side of the marsh at the head of the bay. The beach here dries for a fair distance—great for clam diggers but not so good for gear-laden kayakers on minus tides. The three or four campsites on either end of the beach have their own outhouses and water. Be advised that the walk to the self-registration station is long and arduous (one-half mile up and over the steep hill to the north), whereas it is a 150-yard paddle to the dock just below it, so take care of this detail before you stash your boat.

There are sites above the dock in Reid Harbor, but the only access to the top of this steep shoreline is via the twisting dock ramp—not easy carrying for a kayak. Nonetheless, this access is easier for getting your craft across to Prevost Harbor or the campsites there than the four and one-half-mile paddle via Johns Pass.

As in Reid Harbor, there are campsites above Prevost Harbor's dock and float. But here the bank is lower, and an easy path leads up from the beach next to the dock. The four sites about one hundred yards west are especially appealing, as they have their own beach access. This area also has outhouses and a water faucet.

I strongly suggest allowing a day layover at Stuart Island for some exploration, perhaps to hike the island's ample trails and little-used, unpaved county roads. There are fine opportunities for day-long loops, each skirting the island from one harbor to the other via Johns Pass to the east or Turn Point to the west.

Whichever way you go, note that the currents flow around both ends of the island on their way to or from the Strait of Georgia. With the right timing, both trips can be made with favorable currents for almost the entire distance. See the Canadian *Current Atlas* for specifics.

REID HARBOR TO PREVOST HARBOR VIA JOHNS PASS ONE-DAY LOOP: Protected. The total paddling distance is four and one-half miles. The Johns Pass loop is the easiest and shortest one. Most of this shoreline is residential. Except for Johns Pass, currents along the shore usually are benign, and hence the **protected** rating. The tiny state-owned Gossip Island and Cemetery Island at Reid Harbor's entrance are the only opportunities for shore exploration along this route.

REID HARBOR TO PREVOST HARBOR VIA TURN POINT LOOP: Exposed. The paddling distance is seven miles. I consider the western circuit around Turn Point exceptionally appealing. The wild, rugged shores and boisterous Haro Strait waters provide a setting unmatched in our inland waters. But because of the steep shores with few safe landings, the strong currents that race around the point, and the open north or south fetches with potential for sea development, I rate this loop **exposed.**

From Prevost Harbor, the pastoral civility of Stuart Island is left behind at Charles Point. From there to Turn Point is a progression of rocky kelp beds, sea crags, and overhanging vegetation. Extensive eddies occupy most of these beds all the way to the point, and progress is fairly easy even against the current. These waters are prime fishing grounds for both bottom fish and salmon.

Turn Point is a ten-acre Coast Guard light station reservation surrounded by a fifty-three-acre state park. The light facility is now automated, and the lightkeepers' residences are only occasionally occupied by diverse tenants such as Stuart Island teachers or whale researchers. The park land is undeveloped, with no recreational facilities. Camping is not allowed. It does provide excellent day hiking and it is a popular five-mile hike for boaters from the Reid and Prevost harbors area via an unpaved road.

Turn Point itself provides few easy landing sites for visiting the light station. Though the rocks have eroded into fairly flat shelves, you will have to be adept at landing on rocks in the waves that are usually present. Also beware of the powerful wakes of the ships that pass quite close offshore here.

A much more practical landing with a rough trail access to the point is found at a small gravel beach about one-quarter mile to the south, just beyond some spectacular sea cliffs and still within Turn Point State Park. Secure your boat well above the drift logs and passing freighters' wakes and plan to be gone for at least one hour if you intend to visit the point.

The rough, little-used trail, marked by yellow-green flagging, switchbacks steeply up from the beach. Follow the gully above the beach uphill for about one hundred yards to a more well-defined trail that climbs across the hillside to the left through open fir and madrona woods. This trends upward for another three hundred yards, passing an old oil drum and open grassy meadows above and below, perfect for secluded sunbathing. Finally it reaches a high, bald hilltop with sweeping views over Haro Strait, Boundary Pass, and the Canadian Gulf Islands beyond. Walking down to the cliff edge—be careful—you can see Turn Point light below. A few yards behind this bald hilltop is the old road linking the light station to the Reid and Prevost harbors area. Follow it to the left and downhill to the point.

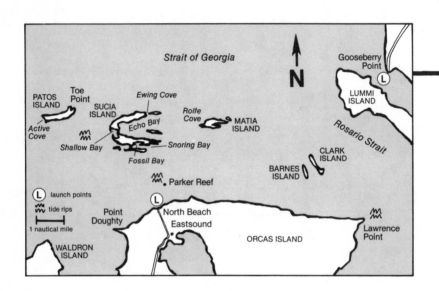

The Northern Rim Islands

North shore of Orcas Island, Patos Island, Sucia Island, Matia Island, and Clark Island

The northern or "Outer Islands" of the San Juan Islands are separated by miles of sea from the islands to the south, and open to the unbroken expanse of the Strait of Georgia to the north. This chain of state park and wildlife refuge islands is famed for its intricate geology as well as its sometimes treacherous waters.

DURATION: Two to four days, depending on route.

RATING: Exposed.

CHARTS AND OTHER NAVIGATION AIDS: NOAA charts 18423 SC or 18421 (both 1:80,000), 18431 and 18430 (both 1:25,000), and San Juan Islands current tables or the Canadian Hydrographic Service's *Current Atlas: Juan de Fuca Strait to Strait of Georgia.*

PLANNING CONSIDERATIONS: This trip puts paddlers at the mercy of the weather, so consult forecasts and be prepared to lay over in the islands during bad weather. Currents are strong throughout the area; avoid spring tides.

Getting There and Launching

From the Orcas Island ferry dock, drive north to Eastsound. At Eastsound, turn north and drive to the end of the road at North Beach. An alternate approach is via Lummi Island from Gooseberry Point (see Lummi Island chapter for directions).

Launch from the gravel beach at the North Beach road end. There is parking for a few cars in the vicinity along the road, but these are usually taken on summer weekends. The nearby Captain Cook Resort accepts parking at $3.00 per car per day.

Routes

CLARK ISLAND VIA GOOSEBERRY POINT AND LUMMI ISLAND: Exposed. The paddling distance is approximately seven miles each way. This approach is most convenient for Bellingham, Washington, or Vancouver, British Columbia, residents. For Seattle-area dwellers, the additional driving time to Lummi Island is probably less than ferry travel to Orcas Island, and certainly it is less expensive. During busy summer weekends, the time saved may amount to one-half day or more. However, the tradeoff comes in longer paddling distances through open waters exposed to the Strait of Georgia to the north and Rosario Strait to the south, with a two-mile crossing to Clark Island from Lummi Island's Village Point, challenged by both swift currents (and possible tide rips) and busy shipping in Rosario Strait (particularly tankers en route to Ferndale's Cherry Point terminal). Currents in this area have no precise secondary reference station in the NOAA current tables. (Station 1635, one and one-half miles north of Clark Island is the closest.) The Canadian *Current Atlas* is most useful for gauging the timing and strength of the current on this crossing.

NORTH BEACH TO SUCIA ISLAND: Exposed. The round-trip paddling distance is approximately six miles. This is the most popular route in this area, involving a weekend-long trip to Sucia Island and pos-

Rock dissolved by sea water on Patos Island.

sible day paddles around the island and to neighboring Matia Island.

The crossing distance from North Beach to the nearest point on Sucia Island is two miles. The greatest hazard en route is Parker Reef, which consists of two separate shoals located less than halfway across. The area around the reefs can develop dangerous rips in strong currents (which can exceed 2 knots), made worse by contrary winds. In September 1985, a kayaking fatality occurred there (reported in *Sea Kayaker* magazine, Winter 1985).

Generally, the west-flowing ebb current is considered the most dangerous. The Canadian *Current Atlas* shows the flood currents coming around the east and west sides of Orcas Island, meeting and weakening in this area. Timing of these currents is somewhat unreliable, and there have been reports of slacks varying greatly from their predicted times. (Using the Canadian *Current Atlas*, I once found the current flow to be the reverse of what was predicted.)

Nonetheless, this route attracts large numbers of paddlers during the summer months, novices included, to the point that I hesitated in giving it the **exposed** rating. However, the potential for risk remains (as the record unfortunately shows), and so does my rating.

NORTH BEACH TO POINT DOUGHTY TO PATOS ISLAND TO CLARK ISLAND TO LAWRENCE POINT: Exposed. The total paddling distance for the entire rectangle is thirty miles, but it can be reduced to about six miles (North Beach to Sucia Island and return) by eliminating the points of call.

Point Doughty on the northwest tip of Orcas Island forms a corner of the rectangle route. Though this is somewhat of a detour en route to the island chain, the recreation area at the point serves as a convenient first-night stop for those getting a late start on the water, or as a place to wait out a day of bad weather before crossing to the islands. The area is a fine destination in itself, with attractive madrona and fir woods, rocks and tide pools at the point, and spectacular cliffs (complete with a small sea cave or two) on the north side. It is a popular area for scuba divers. There are campsites, pit toilets, and garbage cans, but no water.

Access is via a small beach on the south side of the point. At midtide or above, landings are on pebbles and gravel; low tide approaches are rocky and may be hard on the boat if there is a southerly sea running. At this writing, access from the beach to the upland is a bit difficult as the trail has eroded and largely slid down the steep bank.

There are two campsite areas. One has good views to the south and west, but poor weather protection. The other is tucked into the trees and is a good all-weather camp, but without views. Trails lead east from the campsites along the south bluffs and eventually to the YMCA's Camp Orkila one mile to the east. There is no public access by land.

East along Orcas Island's northern shore from Point Doughty.

From Point Doughty, the crossing to Patos Island is slightly over four miles, with strong currents and possible tide rips along the route. A safer but longer alternative is to head for Sucia Island first, and then cut across to Patos Island at the time of the slack. Either route is both safer and far easier on the flood current. Watch for rips in the area of West Bank (which is marked by an extensive kelp bed).

Patos Island is one of the wildest islands in the northern chain. The island is currently owned by the federal government and managed by Washington State Parks, though a transfer to the state is being processed at the time of this writing. Four acres at Alden Point will remain a Coast Guard light station and are presently off-limits to the public.

All developments and camping are confined to the west end of the island, as the remainder is managed to enhance bald eagle nesting habitat. Campsites are located at Active Cove, with pit toilets but no water or garbage service (and no charge for their use). There is a trail across the island from the campsites and part of the way down the north shore to the east.

Patos Island merits a paddling circumnavigation and is the more practical way of seeing this brushy island. On the south shore are bluffs and low cliffs, with the weird eroded conglomerate rocks that characterize this island chain. The east end has two coves with pebble beaches and long rock reefs, which are revealed at low tide a long distance from shore, giving Toe Point its name. These excellent beaches comprise the majority of the northern shoreline.

Sucia Island is the hub of cruising in the northern San Juan Islands, for yachts and kayaks alike. You are least likely to find solitude in the summer on Sucia Island, but other attractions make up for it. This island complex (actually at least six separate islands) can absorb a day's exploring by kayak, and then another by foot along the extensive trail system. The bizarre formations of water-dissolved rock are unsurpassed, and seals abound on and around them.

The majority of visitors to Sucia Island are found in Fossil and Echo bays, where there are extensive campsites with drinking water and solar composting toilets. The low banks and shell and gravel beaches make attractive camping for kayakers in Fossil Bay or in adjoining Fox Cove. Echo Bay or Shallow Bay just across the island to the west have similar camps, with drinking water near the picnic shelter in northern Shallow Bay. All of the campsites in these areas carry a fee levied through self-registration stations. Starting in fall 1985, a "pack-it-out" garbage program was initiated on Sucia Island, and trash cans are no longer provided.

While the Fossil and Echo bay complexes are the best campsites for the off-season (driftwood for fires piles up in Echo Bay during the winter), kayakers visiting Sucia Island during the summer generally prefer Ewing Cove or Snoring Bay for the relative isolation from other boaters and campers that these areas afford. There is no charge for camping at either. Camp only at sites designated with a fire ring and/or a picnic table. Camping elsewhere is *prohibited*, particularly on Little Sucia Island, which is managed as an eagle preserve.

Matia Island, a little more than one mile from Sucia Island, is hard

Ewing Cove on Sucia Island.

pressed to maintain its wild quality in the face of nearby boating activity. In fact, management of the island is something of a dilemma. Matia Island is entirely owned by the federal government as a national wildlife refuge managed for bald eagles and pelagic cormorants, with five acres at Rolfe Cove leased to state parks (which in fact manages the rest of the island too for the U.S. Fish and Wildlife Service). Boaters exploring Matia Island have created an unofficial trail network throughout. Refuge managers plan to improve and mark part of this network and close the remainder to protect particularly sensitive nesting sites.

Camping is confined to Rolfe Cove, which provides well-protected sites above the gravel beach and low bluffs. Though there is a well, water is not provided because it cannot be chlorinated with the hand pump to meet health standards. A new solar composting toilet is nearby. Fees are collected through the self-registration station. Nearby Eagle Cove is outside the state park lease area and closed to camping.

Around Matia Island are numerous coves best visited by boat to comply with refuge objectives. On the south side is "the hermit's cove," where remnants of the solitary island dwellers' structures dating to the 1920s still can be seen. At the southeast corner are coves with more pebble beaches.

Refuge managers ask that you not go ashore in the cove at the east end of the island because of eagle nests located there.

Clark Island is the smallest state park island in the chain. Getting there from Matia Island also involves the longest and most exposed crossing—almost four miles. There is a sand beach on the west side and a gravel one on the east. Camping is allowed only on sites most easily reached from the east beach.

Currents move very swiftly around either end of Clark Island and nearby Barnes Island (privately owned), so watch out for tide rips. The Sisters islands to the southeast of Clark Island are units of San Juan Islands National Wildlife Refuge, and landings are *prohibited*.

Paths circle the low bluffs around the southern end of Clark Island, with open madrona woods onshore and extensive tide pools and tideflats below at low tide. There are no trails to the brushy north end, but rounding the cliffs and offshore rocks is a nice paddling excursion.

Approximately six campsites are spotted along the east beach and are low enough that a loaded kayak can be dragged right into camp. No water is provided on the island, nor is there a camping charge. The beach sites are vulnerable to bad weather; two sites in the woods at the narrowest point of the island are best at those times.

The active currents between Clark Island and Orcas Island make a crossing in this area precarious in unfavorable conditions. On either flood or ebb tides, large eddies form around Lawrence Point and powerful rips may occur at the boundaries with the main current streams. The Canadian *Current Atlas* gives the best picture of the complex flows in this area. Note that strong east-flowing currents move along the shore of Orcas Island on large flood exchanges in this area (the opposite of what you might expect) and flow the same way on large ebbs. Hence, time a crossing to the Lawrence Point area to arrive at slack time and avoid this area on ebbs if southerly winds are likely. Because there are eddies near the point, a close-in route is safest if you

Clark Island.

must pass by while the currents are running. In unsettled weather, I recommend cutting this area out of the rectangle. To avoid it, cross from Barnes Island directly to Orcas Island's shore a mile or more west of Lawrence Point.

Lawrence Point is the optional southeast corner of the rectangle route. The point is DNR school land, and though open to camping, it is not a particularly good place for it. The grassy point does make a pleasant lunch stop or a place to watch the swirling currents and wait for favorable ones. Access is via two narrow pebble beaches on the south side of the point.

The north shore of Orcas Island forms the last six-mile leg of the rectangular route. Though this linear shoreline appears unexciting on the chart, I found it gratifying to follow. There are few spots for an emergency camp, so hope for fair weather during this leg of the journey. Most of the shore is very steep, with either wooded scree slopes or cliffs rising right from sea level. There are occasional narrow gravel beaches at the base but rarely anywhere to go above. Nonetheless, the coast is wild—look for otter and hauled-out seals—and has a few surprise bits of history. At one point there is an old limestone kiln fitted into the steep slope, and so unobtrusive that most other boaters probably miss it. Farther on is an extensive, overgrown quarry now covered by a vigorous young fir forest.

Near the tiny extension of Moran State Park that reaches the sea is a rarity for the San Juan Islands—a waterfall spilling into the sea at high tide. Houses appear during the final third of the way to North Beach.

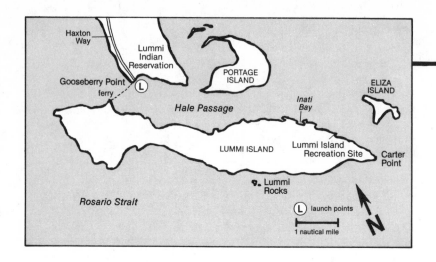

Haxton Way

Lummi Indian Reservation

Gooseberry Point
ferry

PORTAGE ISLAND

Hale Passage

Inati Bay

ELIZA ISLAND

LUMMI ISLAND

Lummi Island Recreation Site

Carter Point

Lummi Rocks

Rosario Strait

Ⓛ launch points

1 nautical mile

N

Lummi Island

Though it has most of the amenities of the San Juan Islands, Lummi Island is sufficiently off the beaten cruising path to be missed by most boaters. The southern end has all the ruggedness that makes along-shore paddling so interesting, and a campground to match.

DURATION: Two days.

RATING: Moderate or Exposed.

CHARTS AND OTHER NAVIGATION AIDS: NOAA charts 18423 SC, 18421 (both 1:80,000) or 18424 (1:40,000), and current tables or the Canadian Hydrographic Service's *Current Atlas: Juan de Fuca Strait to Strait of Georgia.*

PLANNING CONSIDERATIONS: Moderate currents in Hale Passage affect paddling ease along the shores. Very strong currents along Lummi Island's southwest shores can be hazardous against a contrary wind.

Getting There and Launching

From Interstate 5, take Exit 260 (Lummi Island-Slater Road), and turn west onto Slater Road. After almost four miles, turn left onto Haxton Way. Follow Haxton Way for six and one-half miles to the Lummi Island ferry landing at Gooseberry Point.

Park in the lot south of the ferry dock at Gooseberry Point in an out-of-the-way spot so as not to conflict with ferry parking. Launch from the sandy beach next to the dock.

Routes

HALE PASSAGE LOOP: Moderate. The total paddling distance is approximately thirteen miles. This pleasant overnight trip follows Lummi Island's east shore south to a campsite at one of the more interesting DNR recreation sites. Return can be by the same route, or for a little variation and weather permitting, across Hale Passage to Portage Island for the return to Gooseberry Point.

Although the crossing from Gooseberry Point to Lummi Point is only about two-thirds of a mile, swift currents of up to 2 knots can make paddling to the opposite shore exhausting, and it can be dangerous in winds opposing the current. Hence, time this crossing for near the slack, and then catch the ebb down Lummi Island's shore if possible. Though the along-shore currents are not terribly swift, they are persistent and tiring against a contrary tide.

Northern Lummi Island is a mixture of farms and residences. There is little wild shoreline on the northern half on either side of the island. Along Hale Passage, homes become sparser as you come abreast of Portage Island on the opposite shore. They gradually diminish as the shoreline steepens and disappear altogether just north of Inati Bay. At that point there is also a gravel pit with an interesting old ship's hulk in use as a pier to dock barges against. Round that last point, and you will find that Lummi Island is wild to the south.

Inati Bay is a fine spot for a stretch onshore, though it is likely that there will be boats moored there during the cruising season. The Bellingham Yacht Club leases the head of the bay for a boaters' shore stop and has installed pit toilets and fire rings. The woods behind are well worth a walk inland, and there is an old road that eventually leads to the main road from the north.

Lummi Island Recreation Site is less than one mile south of Inati Bay, beyond gradually steepening rocky shores. This DNR site is a particularly interesting one, as it is essentially carved into a steep hillside. Steps and switchbacking trails connect two tiny coves to upland campsites, which make use of every level spot. The result is a charming campsite, which is especially attractive to kayakers because it provides poor moorage for other boats with no protection against southerly blows. The campsites are more secluded than those at other such recreation areas, making this a nice place to stay even if others are present. As with other DNR sites, there is no water service, but garbage cans and pit toilets are provided.

At this point, this particular route turns back to the north. It is here that you can opt to cross Hale Passage to Portage Island for the return to Gooseberry Point. Portage Island, part of the Lummi Indian Reservation, is quite wild with beaches fronting on woods and meadows beyond. The island is connected to the mainland by a spit that dries at midtide, and cars frequently drive across it.

LUMMI ISLAND CIRCUMNAVIGATION: Exposed. The total paddling distance is approximately nineteen miles. Venturing south toward Carter Point or around to the southwest side of Lummi Island takes you into a world of unforgiving rocky shorelines. There are few opportunities for anything but an uncomfortable emergency bivouac should

Two of the three coves at Lummi Island Recreation site.

the weather turn against you. After rounding the point, the shoreline is a continuous scree slope punctuated by cliffs that rise abruptly to the ridgeline, which gradually ascends toward 1,600-foot Lummi Peak as you move north. There are few haul outs until passing opposite Lummi Rocks, and then the country gradually flattens, and pastoral and residential developments take over again.

There are no established campsites on this western route, so get an early start from the DNR site, provided good weather and favorable currents (which sweep strongly against Lummi Island's southwest shores) prevail.

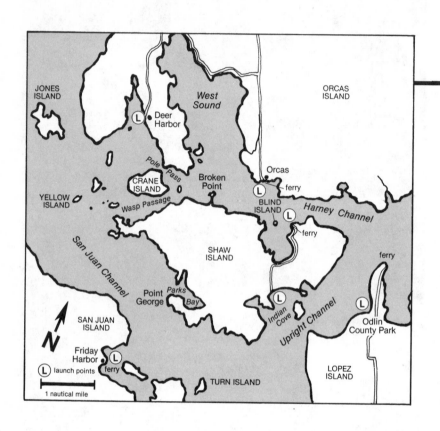

Central San Juan Islands

Shaw Island, Jones Island, and Turn Island

Located in the protected heartland of the San Juan Islands, this area usually has the highest concentrations of kayaks in the islands. Moderate currents and along-shore paddling with few crossings make it popular for less experienced paddlers. But avoid holiday weekends here—you may not be able to find a campsite.

DURATION: Two to three days.

RATING: Moderate.

CHARTS AND OTHER NAVIGATION AIDS: NOAA charts 18423 SC or 18421 (both 1:80,000), and 18434 (1:25,000). Current tables or the Canadian Hydrographic Service's *Current Atlas: Juan de Fuca Strait to Strait of Georgia* in particular are useful for route timing. A tide table is handy if Indian Cove is included as a launch point or stop.

PLANNING CONSIDERATIONS: Timing with currents will greatly affect your speed and travel effort. Plan your arrival or departure at Indian Cove around low tides to avoid the mud flats there.

Getting There and Launching

To reach the San Juan Islands, exit Interstate 5 at Burlington and follow Highway 20 to Anacortes. Continue approximately four miles, following signs to the San Juan Islands ferry terminal. Take the ferry to Lopez Island, Shaw Island, or Orcas Island, depending on the launch site selected. A launch from Lopez Island saves time en route as there are no intermediate ferry stops.

To launch from Lopez Island, drive to Odlin County Park, a little more than one mile south of the ferry terminal. There is easy access to the sandy beach, and cars may be parked for $2.00 per day. This is probably the most convenient launch point for the Shaw Island loop.

To launch from Orcas Island, drive to the town of Orcas. Launch

The Wasp Islands.

from the float at Russell's just west of the ferry dock. There is a $5.00 fee for using the float. The fee includes the haul out. Parking may be very difficult to find in this area during the busy summer months.

To launch at Deer Harbor, Orcas Island, drive to the Deer Harbor Marina and Resort. There is a $5.00 fee for launching, plus $5.00 per day for parking. Do not get your drinking water in Deer Harbor—it tastes terrible.

To launch from Shaw Island, drive to the county park at Indian Cove (South Beach). There is easy access to the sandy beach via the ramp at the east end of the park, but the low tide uncovers a long, mucky tideflat that makes for a difficult and unpleasant launch. Park along the road up the hill in the camping area.

Do *not* park at the Shaw Island ferry landing. Though launching is permitted at the beach just to the west, there is not sufficient room for kayakers to park here. The Franciscan nuns operate a store at the landing that has a surprisingly extensive grocery selection.

It is also possible to launch from Friday Harbor on San Juan Island for a Shaw Island circumnavigation. See the Stuart Island chapter for a description of this launch point.

Routes

SHAW ISLAND CIRCUMNAVIGATION: Moderate. The total paddling distance is approximately fourteen miles. Add two miles for a side trip to Turn Island or three miles to Jones Island. Add two miles if you launch from Deer Harbor. Harney Channel, separating northeastern Shaw Island from Orcas Island, is a fairly mild and protected waterway with weak currents. Watch for ferries and their wakes here and on almost all of this route. The Shaw Island side is the least developed. In all of the waterways between Orcas Island and Shaw Island, hugging the shorelines is probably the most advisable route, both because it is interesting (for instance, the cliffs at Broken Point) and to avoid the heavy boating traffic in these passages.

At the Shaw Island ferry landing, you may land on the beach just right of the dock (*do not* use the floats left of the dock) for a visit to the nuns' store. Be careful about creating congestion here, and be conscious of not aggravating past conflicts that the nuns have had with kayakers. (Vehicle congestion and prohibited launches from the floats have been their major complaints.)

Blind Island is one of the smallest state parks on which camping is allowed. Sites are primitive, with no water and a single outhouse. There is no camping fee. Landings can be made on rocky beaches at the southwest end or at the southeast corner of the island. Trees on the island are few, and the only wind protection is chest-high brush that shields some of the sites. Because of its small size, Blind Island becomes crowded with only a few parties camped there; go elsewhere if you want solitude.

Continue along Shaw Island to the west of Blind Bay to Broken Point, where you will choose a route depending on whether you are going to Jones Island. For Jones Island, you will probably want to cross here to Orcas Island and head for Pole Pass.

Pole Pass is a little tide race that can run at more than 2 knots for a short distance. It is rarely dangerous, but boat wakes in the riffles on the downstream side can make it quite rough. It is possible to go through against the current, as it is quite weak in the approaches. There are eddies on the Orcas Island shore, which require a hard push for a short distance in the narrows against the flow. Be especially wary of boat traffic in Pole Pass, as it is difficult to see what is coming the other way as you approach.

Jones Island State Park is a very popular destination for kayakers and other boaters—so popular that campsites are difficult to find on summer weekends. Most boaters prefer the more protected northern cove, where there is a dock. Kayakers like the southern beach or a smaller one on the northwest side of the island, though southerly wind protection is slight at most of the campsites in these areas. There are numerous sites at both the northern or southern areas, and one on the west side. From the west beach, a two-hundred-yard trail leads to the north camp area. At all locations, only sites designated with a numbered picnic table may be used for camping. All of these sites carry a $3.00 fee levied through the self-registration stations at the north and south ends. Though drinking water faucets are provided at both places, the shallow well usually runs dry in midsummer, and the water is shut off between October and March (camping fees are not in effect at this time).

The Wasp Islands to the south of Jones Island are another favorite. The scattering of islands and rocks make for interesting and scenic paddling. Most of the Wasp Islands are privately owned, and a few smaller ones are part of the national wildlife refuge in which landings are *prohibited*.

Currents in this area are moderate. Wasp Passage runs swiftly enough to produce rips in the area of Crane Island. The major hazard here is the ferry, which takes this route between Friday Harbor and Orcas Island. It can come around the corner quite suddenly from either direction, so do not dawdle in midchannel at Wasp Passage. Also watch out for ferry wakes colliding with an opposing current (that is, when the ferry is traveling against the current), as these can become steep and nasty breakers. The wakes will smooth out after entering the eddies along the sides of the passage.

The Shaw Island shore of Wasp Passage is a fine place to practice using shore eddies to travel against the current, if you need to do so. Note that the currents in this area run counter to what might be expected. They flow west into San Juan Channel on the flood tide.

Yellow Island, owned by The Nature Conservancy, is managed to perpetuate the island's unique floral communities. The main attraction is the spring flowers, which begin in late March and are at their best

Yellow Island.

from mid-April through early summer. Resident caretakers live in the cabin on the southwest shore.

Kayakers should be aware that Yellow Island is *not* a public park, and that visits are permitted only under stringent conditions to insure that the primary goal of preservation is not compromised. Stops here should be short and only for the purpose of viewing the island. Stay on the trail that meanders around it. Collecting plants or intertidal life, smoking, pets, camping, picnicking, and fires are *prohibited*, and there are no public toilets. The Nature Conservancy management has been concerned about kayakers using the meadows as toilets, and the island may be closed to kayak groups if the problem continues. Groups of more than six individuals must have prior permission to visit Yellow Island by calling The Nature Conservancy in Seattle at 728-9696.

Along Shaw Island's western shore, the San Juan Channel current can be quite strong, especially at the points that protrude into the waterway. Along shore, there are eddy systems for much of the way, with extensive eddies in the vicinity of Parks Bay. Though most of the northern portion of this shore is developed with summer residences, there are some points of interest. The small islands just south of the Neck Point peninsula are very popular with seals—I have seen as many as thirty hauled out on the islands.

Beginning at Point George is a one thousand-plus-acre biological preserve owned by the University of Washington, which extends south and west almost to Squaw Bay. Managed by the University of Washington Friday Harbor Laboratories, the preserve is used primarily for studies of intertidal ecology and landscape architecture in the uplands. Green and white signs along the shore identify the preserve, and prohibit hunting, camping, fires, and dogs. You may go ashore in the intertidal zone here to stretch your legs, but not into the uplands. Avoid any markers that identify study plots, and do not go ashore at all where there are yellow signs to that effect.

Turn Island State Park, located a little over one mile south of Shaw Island across San Juan Channel, provides another side trip opportunity for either a brief stop or overnight camping. This island is a unit of the San Juan Islands National Wildlife Refuge. A portion of the west end is leased to Washington State Parks. Camping is allowed only in this park area. Fees are levied through the self-registration station. There are composting toilets, but water is not available.

A rough trail, which the Fish and Wildlife Service plans to improve and reroute, circles the island. Keep in mind that public use of this refuge island is provisional on compatibility with wildlife, so avoid any nesting sites.

Be careful crossing San Juan Channel here. Currents are strong enough to require significant course adjustment to offset your drift, and steep seas can develop when the current opposes winds from either north or south. Watch for ferries and other heavy boat traffic associated with nearby Friday Harbor.

In general, Upright Channel has the weaker currents of the waterways around Shaw Island, with the exception of the south tip of the island and at the narrows between Canoe Island and Lopez Island. There are no reference stations for this channel in the current tables. The flood current flows north.

Indian Cove has a county park with opportunities for camping or simply a stop ashore. Because the foreshore here dries for a considerable distance and becomes a muddy tideflat, plan around low tides for arrival and departure if possible.

Campsites are located along a road starting along a low bank to the east and climbing as the bank increases to a bluff to the west. There are steps at intervals along the beach to the campsites, but the most westerly ones are not readily accessible from the water. The fee for a campsite with up to four people is $6.00 and $1.50 for each additional individual. If you wish to share a site with others (and you may have to during peak weekends), there is a shared camp area just west of Campsite 9, which costs $1.50 per person. Water, pit toilets, and a cooking shelter are provided.

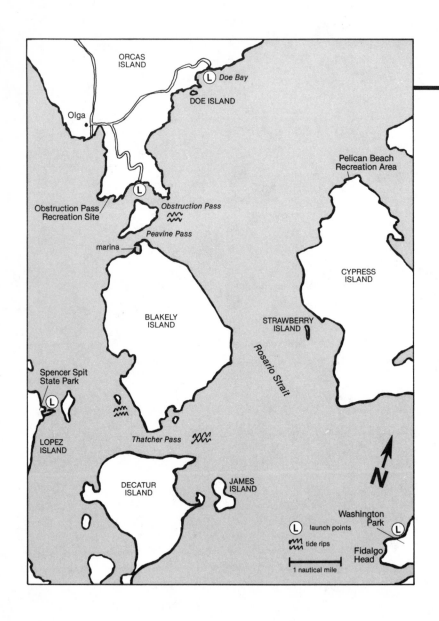

ORCAS
ISLAND

L *Doe Bay*

DOE ISLAND

Olga

Pelican Beach
Recreation Area

Obstruction Pass
Recreation Site

L

Obstruction Pass

Peavine Pass

marina

CYPRESS
ISLAND

BLAKELY
ISLAND

STRAWBERRY
ISLAND

Rosario Strait

Spencer Spit
State Park

L

LOPEZ
ISLAND

Thatcher Pass

DECATUR
ISLAND

JAMES
ISLAND

N

Washington
Park

L launch points

tide rips

Fidalgo
Head

L

1 nautical mile

Western Rosario Strait

Eastern Orcas Island, Blakely Island, and James Island

This area of the San Juan Islands receives fewer kayak visitors than others, primarily because it is more difficult to reach. But the scenery and marine parks are among the best the islands have to offer.

DURATION: One to three days.

RATING: Moderate to Exposed.

CHARTS AND OTHER NAVIGATION AIDS: NOAA charts 18423 SC or 18421 (both 1:80,000), 18430 (1:25,000), and current tables.

PLANNING CONSIDERATIONS: There are strong currents in Thatcher, Peavine, and Obstruction passes, all flowing westerly on flood currents.

Getting There and Launching

For the Washington Park launch in Anacortes, exit Interstate 5 at Burlington and follow Highway 20 to Anacortes. Continue approximately four miles, following signs to the San Juan Islands ferry terminal. At the top of the hill above the ferry terminal, continue straight at the Y where ferry traffic bears right and go another one-half mile to Washington Park. Park in the overnight lot above the playground (designated "Lot A"), or at the Y behind the park entrance sign. To get closest to the beach, drive down to the day-use parking area to unload, and then move your car to an overnight lot.

For the Obstruction Pass and Doe Bay launches on Orcas Island, follow the above instructions to the San Juan Islands ferry terminal. The launch sites are approximately twenty miles from the ferry landing on Orcas Island. Follow the road to Eastsound and then to Olga. Approximately one-quarter mile before Olga, turn left (signs point to Obstruction Pass and Doe Bay). After another one-quarter mile there is a fork in the road; go right for Obstruction Pass and left for Doe Bay.

To launch from the ramp at Obstruction Pass, use the access to a sandy beach. The problem with this launch site is the lack of overnight parking. The lot next to the ramp is signed for day parking only (except for a few spaces for Blakely Island and Obstruction Island residents). Though this has not been tightly enforced in the past, you risk being towed away if you leave your car here overnight or if you park along the highway. The only alternative is to try to make an arrangement with a local resident.

To launch from the Doe Bay Village Resort on Orcas Island use the dock. There is no charge for launching from the dock, but parking at the resort is $3.00 per vehicle per day. Camping is available. There are showers, hot tubs, and a communal kitchen. The resort also furnishes kayaks for short guided tours of the local area.

For the Spencer Spit State Park launch on Lopez Island, follow the above instructions to the San Juan Islands ferry terminal. On Lopez Island drive south from the ferry landing a little more than one mile to Port Stanley Road (across the highway from Odlin County Park). Turn

The southern shore of James Island.

left here and follow this road for approximately three miles as it winds past Shoal and Swifts bays. Turn left onto Baker View Road and follow this road another mile to the state park entrance.

To launch from Spencer Spit State Park on Lopez Island use the gravel road to the right at the park office to reach the beach. This narrow road drops steeply to a small lot just south of the lagoon. There is a fifty-yard carry remaining to the beach. After unloading boats and gear, move cars back up to the main road, then go right to the parking lot and park just past the rest room on the left. The ranger asks that you leave a "float plan" with him or on your car in case of emergency.

Route

BLAKELY ISLAND CIRCUMNAVIGATION: Moderate. The total paddling distance including a stop at James Island is approximately fourteen miles. Add five miles for the round trip from Doe Bay, or four miles for the round trip to Spencer Spit. Though currents on the west side of Blakely Island are weak, they are strong in Thatcher, Peavine, and Obstruction passes and along the east side of Blakely Island in Rosario Strait, so plan the trip accordingly. These passes do not merit waiting for slack current, but they can develop dangerous breaking seas when running in either direction against opposing winds. The current along Blakely Island's east shore is reported to turn to the flood an hour later than Rosario Strait.

Though almost entirely privately owned and operated for second homeowners, Blakely Island still is largely wild and is impressively rugged. The east shore is very steep, with few landing possibilities should you require them, so plan to stick to the more protected west side if the weather should turn unpleasant. The west side is almost as precipitous. Plan on staying in your boat for both of these four- to six-mile passages, bracketed by either James Island or Spencer Spit to the south or Blakely Island Marina or Obstruction Pass Recreation Site to the north. There are no rest room or lunch breaks en route.

Doe Island State Park is a short paddle from Doe Bay Village Resort and a good overnight destination if you made a late start from the latter. Landings on the rocky beaches are not especially easy here when the float is removed during the off-season; the best are at the southeast end (watch for big tanker wakes breaking on the beaches here) or on the northwest shore. Camping is primitive. There are pit toilets but water is not available.

The DNR's Obstruction Pass Recreation Site lies in a cove on Orcas Island about one-half mile west of the pass. This camp and picnic area is also accessible from the road via a one-half-mile-long trail.

Obstruction Pass Recreation Site.

Above the pebble beach are the agency's usual primitive campsites and pit toilets, but no water.

Blakely Island Marina at the west end of Peavine Pass has the only groceries on this route. The store operates on limited hours during the off-season. Land on the beach to the left of the fuel float.

At the southern end of the loop, Spencer Spit State Park is an attractive diversion for either camping or a stop to walk its beaches or paddle into the lagoon at high tide. Fifteen campsites for boaters or walk-in campers are located along the northern beach. The fee is $3.00. Water and rest rooms are available.

James Island State Park is a destination in its own right. There are three camping areas, a network of trails, and a secluded beach on the south shore. Its drawback is the rapacious raccoon population that lurks in wait for all visitors.

Campsites are accessible from either the eastern or western coves. The fee is $3.00 during the summer season, but water is not available on the island. The central area between the coves is the most popular with boaters, and it has a small picnic shelter. A drawback of camping here is the winds that can howl across the isthmus from either direction. On the east side, camps at the southern side of the cove offer more protection but have few level spots for tents. The three secluded sites at the southern side of the west cove are the most popular with kayakers. The trees that surround these sites also make them the best protected in bad weather. Beyond the pit toilet, a trail leads across the island to the eastern cove.

The approach to this route from Fidalgo Head across Rosario Strait merits an **exposed** rating. The crossing from the head to James Island is slightly less than three miles. Currents in the straits can exceed 2.5 knots, and they are usually considerably stronger on the ebb than on the flood. Hence, southerly winds can make this an extremely dangerous body of water on a falling tide, and tanker and tug-and-barge traffic add to the hazards. Crossings should be made only in auspicious conditions; otherwise, use the San Juan Islands ferry.

Since your drift from the current will be considerable in all but very small tides, start the crossing about one-half hour before slack so that the currents will be minimal and will cancel each other out before and after the slack. Currents are particularly swift off Fidalgo Head.

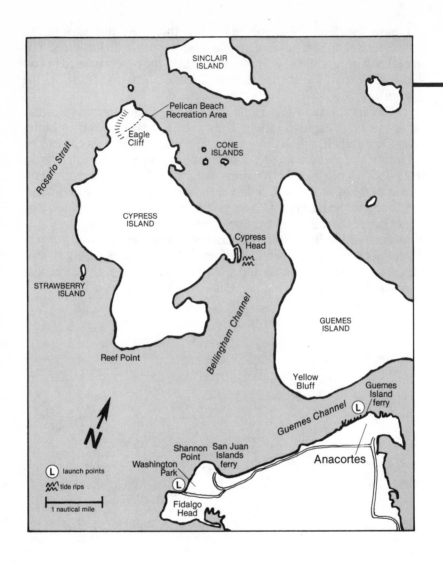

SINCLAIR
ISLAND

Pelican Beach
Recreation Area

Eagle
Cliff

CONE
ISLANDS

Rosario Strait

CYPRESS
ISLAND

Cypress
Head

STRAWBERRY
ISLAND

GUEMES
ISLAND

Reef Point

Bellingham Channel

Yellow
Bluff

Guemes
Island
ferry

Guemes Channel

N

Ⓛ launch points

〰 tide rips

1 nautical mile

Shannon
Point

San Juan
Islands
ferry

Washington
Park

Ⓛ

Anacortes

Fidalgo
Head

Cypress Island

The wild ruggedness of Cypress Island, the chance for a hike to catch the panoramic views from Eagle Cliff, and the three public campsites almost evenly spaced around the island all contribute to its popularity with kayakers. And, ferry trips are not required.

DURATION: Two to three days.

RATING: Moderate + .

CHARTS AND OTHER NAVIGATION AIDS: NOAA charts 18423 SC or 18421 (both 1:80,000), 18430 (1:25,000), and current tables or the Canadian Hydrographic Service's *Current Atlas: Juan de Fuca Strait to Strait of Georgia.*

PLANNING CONSIDERATIONS: This is one of the most popular routes in the San Juan Islands, and campsites may not be available on weekends during the peak season. Strong currents can create very dangerous localized conditions off Cypress Head in Bellingham Channel; avoid spring tides and aim for slack current in this area. Currents strongly affect traveling speeds on all sides of the island; generally, use floods for going north and ebbs for the return.

Getting There and Launching

To launch from Guemes Island ferry landing in Anacortes, exit Interstate 5 at Burlington and follow Highway 20 to Anacortes. In Anacortes, drive north on Commercial Avenue through the intersection where the San Juan Islands ferry traffic normally turns left. Continue to the next light and turn left on 8th Street. Go one block to the stop sign, then continue straight for approximately one-quarter mile. Turn right on 1st Avenue and go two blocks to the ferry landing. Park in the unpaved lot just west of the ferry lot, and launch on the sand and rock beach.

To launch from Washington Park in Anacortes, follow the above directions for Anacortes and then follow signs to the San Juan Islands ferry terminal—approximately four miles. At the top of the hill above the ferry terminal continue straight at the Y where ferry traffic bears right, and go another one-half mile to Washington Park. Overnight

Rosario Strait and Cypress Island.

parking is allowed in the lot above the playground (designated "Lot A"), or at the Y behind the park entrance sign. To get closest to the beach, drive down to the day-use parking area to unload, and then move your car to an overnight lot. At present there is no charge for overnight parking, but it is probable in the future.

Route

CYPRESS ISLAND CIRCUMNAVIGATION: Moderate + . The total paddling distance is approximately fifteen miles. Use the Canadian *Current Atlas* to visualize and plan your trip around the currents in Bellingham and Guemes channels and in Rosario Strait. The stage of the tide affects which launch point is the more practical for starting out at that time.

The launch point at the Guemes Island ferry landing is probably safer and more versatile for starts at different tide stages than the Washington Park put-in near Fidalgo Head. Currents sweep strongly around this body of land, and the crossing from there to Cypress Island is more than two miles. As the ebb current sets southwest, reaching Cypress Island from the Fidalgo Head/Shannon Point area on even average tides can be almost impossible. There is a good possibility of being swept out into Rosario Strait in the process. This situation also would be very rough with a southerly wind.

On strong ebb currents, the Guemes Island ferry launch offers both a safer and an easier option. Cross the one-half-mile-wide Guemes Channel (usually possible on most tide stages), and then work west along Guemes Island and up its west shore. Wait until the current slacks before crossing Bellingham Channel to Cypress Island.

On flood currents, Washington Park may be an easier launch point, as the current flowing northward can be ridden into Bellingham Channel. From the Guemes Island ferry landing, you will have to fight the east-flowing flood current (though it generally is weaker than the ebb) in Guemes Channel until rounding the corner into Bellingham Channel.

Midway up Bellingham Channel is Cypress Head. This protuberance creates back eddies, strong eddy lines, and associated rips that can be very dangerous, particularly on large ebb tides. In May 1984, a stable double kayak capsized in this turbulence, and the paddlers were lucky to be rescued after a considerable time in the water (see *Sea Kayaker* magazine, Summer/Fall 1984). Avoid this area during strong currents, especially spring ebb tides. If you approach while the current is flowing, hug the shoreline. The back eddy extends one hundred feet off Cypress Head, and the safest route is right along the shore inside the kelp.

Cypress Head is a DNR Recreation Site with campsites in the woods on the head or at the neck connecting it to the main island—a great place to watch the action in a big ebb exchange. Landings are at the rock and gravel beaches on either the north or south sides of the neck. (You will also find a dock and float on the north side during the warmer months.) The three sites on the west end of the neck are the most convenient from the beaches, but the more distant sites in the

Bellingham Channel.

woods offer better weather protection. There are the usual pit toilets, but water is not available.

About one-half mile east of the northern end of Cypress Island is Pelican Beach, another DNR area developed with help from the Pelican Fleet (owners of a type of beachable cruising sailboat, which are often found hauled up on this fine pebble beach). One of the nicest features here is Eagle Cliff, a spectacular 840-foot overlook of the entire Rosario Strait area. The trail is a little more than one mile long. The climb is easy except for the last few hundred yards. The open meadowed uplands around Eagle Cliff invite independent exploration (be careful of the sheer drops), and there is an alternative loop to another overlook.

At the beach there is camping space for about four groups, and though more can be accommodated, the narrow beach strip quickly becomes crowded (mostly with kayakers). Behind is a covered picnic shelter and pit toilets (water is not available).

The currents along the Rosario Strait side of Cypress Island are strong enough to merit planning around them, though there are enough eddies in this irregular shoreline to work against them for most of the distance. Topography here is at its most impressive; Eagle Cliff and other precipices are far above.

Strawberry Island is yet another DNR recreation area that provides simple campsites along the southwest side of this one-quarter-mile-long island. Access is via a small beach at the south end, which is gravel at high tide but rocky at low water. As elsewhere along Rosario Strait, be wary of huge breaking wakes from passing tankers when you beach your boat.

Camps are up to one hundred yards north; those with the best weather protection are the most distant. A trail continues north up the island to an overlook.

From Reef Point at Cypress Island's southern end, formulate tactics for crossing to Fidalgo Island (if that is your destination) with the powerful offshore currents in mind. On a flood tide, crossing to the Washington Park area can be exhausting or even impossible. Ebbs, however, make this easy (barring southerly winds), with some course correction to counteract westerly drift. If you are bound for Guemes Channel, use a slack or flood current to cross to Yellow Bluff on Guemes Island and then get a lift from the flood up Guemes Channel to the ferry landing.

Places to Go—
North Puget Sound

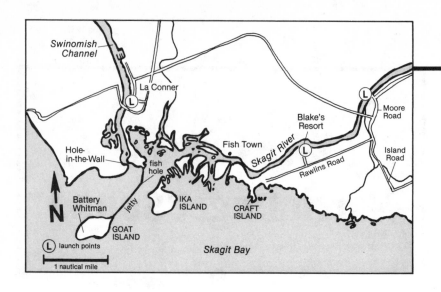

Skagit River Delta

The Skagit River Delta is a birder's paradise and more. A maze of marshland channels, river dwellers' shanties and floathouses, and even overgrown pre-World War II coast artillery emplacements are included in the rich estuary country within the Skagit Wildlife Area.

DURATION: Day trip only. The number of hours depends on tides and route.

RATING: Protected.

CHARTS AND OTHER NAVIGATION AIDS: NOAA chart 18423 SC (1:80,000), or USGS 7.5 Minute Series (1:24,000) Topographic map for the Utsalady Quadrangle.

PLANNING CONSIDERATIONS: Midtide or higher (at least four feet above mean low water) is required for paddling outside the Skagit River channel and Swinomish Channel. Both the river and the Swinomish Channel reverse their currents with the tide (at least one hour after the tide change) and affect paddling effort to and from all launch locations. You may wish to avoid the heavy bird-hunting period from mid-September through December; contact the Department of Game for specifics.

Getting There and Launching

From Interstate 5 take the La Conner-Conway exit and branch right to Conway soon after. Continue about five miles on Fir Island Road. For the lower river launch at Blake's Skagit Resort and Marina, turn left on Rawlins Road. The turnoff for the upper river launch site is one-third mile beyond Rawlins Road, just before the North Fork bridge. Take the turnoff straight onto Moore Road, then take the first unsigned dirt road to the left one-quarter mile beyond at the S-curve.

Blake's Skagit Resort and Marina, approximately one mile above the delta area, is the lowest launch point on the North Fork of the Skagit River. The resort charges $2.50 per kayak, which covers both put-in and take-out. Groups of six boats or more may work out a discount. There is ample parking at no additional cost.

The Department of Game boat launch is located approximately

One-half mile from shore in the lower Skagit delta.

one and one-half river miles above Blake's. After the turnoff from Moore Road, take the right fork on the dirt road.

To launch from La Conner follow the above directions and continue five miles beyond the S-curve. The La Conner public boat ramp is located below and just north of the Rainbow Bridge. After entering La Conner, turn left on Maple, then right on Caledonia Street, left on 2nd, and finally right on Sherman Street. The ramp is straight ahead at the waterfront. There is a $1.00 fee for use of the ramp for both put-in and take-out. Park in the lot across the street or along the street beyond.

Routes

SKAGIT RIVER TO CRAFT ISLAND IN THE DELTA AND RETURN: Protected. The paddling distance is three to five miles each way. Time your start to ensure that you will have mid- to high tide in the delta area once you get downriver. The distance from Blake's to the shallow delta area is about one and one-half miles and about three miles from the upper river launch. There is a downstream current from both launches during the ebb, and an upstream flow as far as the upper launch on larger flood tides (though this begins as much as hours after low tide).

Craft Island is really a hill jutting up from an otherwise flat marsh and tidelands to the west of the river as it nears the mouth. From the top is a sweeping panorama of the marshlands to the north and south and, at low tide, the vast gray tideflats to the west. This and the other upland islands are particularly sensitive habitat for raptors, including bald eagles and red-tailed hawks. If you go ashore, avoid approaching or disturbing these birds, particularly the nesting sites in use.

Timing for the Craft Island excursion is important, as the side channel to it is dry below midtide. If you have the time, you may wish to head downriver at early ebb, paddle to the island, and spend the last of the ebb and early flood lunching, exploring, or just enjoying the view.

Heading downriver approximately one mile below Blake's, you reach a sharp bend to the right and just beyond are pastoral farm buildings and river dwellers' houses and shacks on the right bank—the community of Fish Town. Just downstream on the left is the first side channel into the delta. Take this channel for Craft Island and keep bearing left (the distance is a little more than a mile after leaving the river).

If your tide timing was off for paddling to Craft Island, you can walk there after returning to the launch point. Drive to the end of Rawlins Road beyond Blake's. A rough trail accessible on lower tides leads across the marsh meadows to the island (about three-quarters of a mile each way).

LA CONNER TO GOAT ISLAND TO SKAGIT DELTA: Protected.
The total paddling distance is seven miles for the loop; additional side trips are possible. Most of this loop can be paddled at tide heights of three feet or more. (Avoiding low tide is not as critical here as for the Craft Island route.) However, at the lower end of the tide you would be scooping sand much of the way in a foot or less of water; getting out to wade and tow your boat may prove easier in spots. Spending the low-tide interval exploring Goat Island would be worthwhile if you can afford the time.

From the public launch at La Conner, follow the channel south through the twisting narrows of Hole-in-the Wall. Beyond, the channel opens to flats with intertidal islets and shallow waterways that invite exploration if the tide is in. To the north is a log-storage area bounded by a stone jetty extending to Goat Island. The route later returns through a tiny gap in this jetty.

Goat Island is large. It has both the dense forest and the grassy meadows with madrona trees that are typical of the more arid San Juan Islands. On the northwest end is Battery Whitman, a component of the extensive coast artillery defenses to Puget Sound built at the turn of the century. There are mounts for three guns in the emplacements, with associated rooms, tunnels, and chambers similar to those found at Fort Warden State Park and Fort Casey State Park. Such defenses had be-

Battery Whitman on the western end of Goat Island.

come obsolete by World War II, when aircraft became more effective than coast artillery against invading fleets. Most of Goat Island was ceded to the state a few years after the war.

To reach the emplacements, look for the old dock along the island's north shore. Behind it is a rocky, muddy beach and the start of a rough trail that climbs to the right. Follow this about 250 yards to the battery.

As with the other islands in the Skagit Wildlife Area, this is a particularly sensitive habitat for resident raptors. The Department of Game asks that you respect the privacy of these birds, particularly during spring nesting. As elsewhere within the Skagit Wildlife Area, no camping is allowed.

Paddling around the south side of Goat Island brings you into the shallowest part of this route, though enough water can be found in the shifting channels of the Skagit River on all but the lowest tides. On ebb tides and the first portion of floods, downstream currents will make moving up into the delta hard and slow work, with few eddies to take advantage of.

At this point, you could take time to explore the many sloughs off the Skagit River's channel and perhaps even cut through the delta to Craft Island about two miles to the east if the tide is high enough.

The return to Swinomish Channel from the Skagit River is via the "fish hole" in the jetty—a small opening allowing migrating salmon that made a wrong turn into Swinomish Channel to get back to the river. Located about two hundred yards from the eastern end of the jetty, this gap is not visible as you approach from upriver, but follow the jetty and you will find it. The hole is dry below midtide.

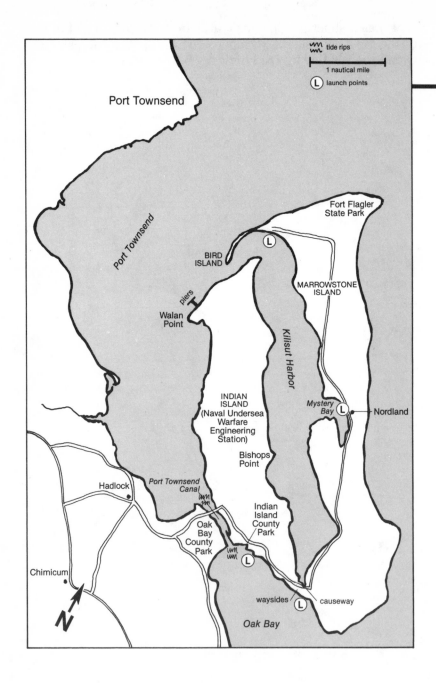

tide rips

1 nautical mile

Ⓛ launch points

Port Townsend

Fort Flagler
State Park

Port Townsend

BIRD
ISLAND

Ⓛ

MARROWSTONE
ISLAND

piers

Walan
Point

Killisut Harbor

INDIAN
ISLAND
(Naval Undersea
Warfare
Engineering
Station)

Mystery
Bay

Ⓛ Nordland

Bishops
Point

Hadlock

Port Townsend
Canal

Indian
Island
County
Park

Oak
Bay
County
Park

Chimicum

waysides Ⓛ causeway

Oak Bay

N

Indian Island

Bands of seals, Navy ships, weird nodules in sandstone formations, a fast sluice through a four-foot-high culvert, all this and more are
found along Indian Island's shores. This naval base won a conservation
award for management of its wildlands, but "look, do not touch":
landing is not allowed. No matter, there are a lot of fine opportunities to
land elsewhere along the route.

DURATION: Day trip only, six to eight hours maximum.

RATING: Moderate, Protected.

CHARTS AND OTHER NAVIGATION AIDS: NOAA charts 18423
SC (1:80,000), 18471 (1:40,000), or 18464 (1:20,000), tide table for Port
Townsend, and current table (see corrections for Port Townsend
Canal).

PLANNING CONSIDERATIONS: Coordinating your launch time
with the tides will dramatically reduce your carrying distance at the
Marrowstone-Indian Island causeway and will aid in catching favorable
currents. At low tide the portage is at least three hundred yards of tideflats; high tide reduces it to as little as fifty feet.

Getting There and Launching

From the Port Townsend highway in Chimacum, turn west at the
blinking yellow light and drive to Hadlock. Turn right at the stop sign in
Hadlock, and then bear left after eight-tenths of a mile to Indian Island.

To launch from Indian Island County Park drive approximately
three-quarters of a mile beyond the Indian Island bridge. Ample parking is available there, with launching on sand or gravel beaches, which
are dry for a considerable distance at low tide. (This also is a popular
clamming spot.)

To launch near the Marrowstone-Indian Island causeway use the
county park waysides. This is probably the most suitable start for the Indian Island circumnavigation, if the launch is at high tide. There are a
series of wayside turnoffs and paths to the beach on Oak Bay to the
south between Indian Island County Park and the causeway. One on
the right, about two-tenths of a mile before the causeway, has off-

Indian Island north of Port Townsend Canal.

highway parking and a short path giving access to the Kilisut Harbor tideflats. This is best for a high-tide launch starting to the north, or for access to the beach on Oak Bay.

To launch from Nordland on Marrowstone Island use the Mystery Bay Recreation Area. This state park area has ample parking and easy access to a sand and gravel beach.

To launch from Fort Flagler State Park at the north end of Marrowstone Island, use the boat launch area on Kilisut Harbor. There is parking and easy access to sand and gravel beaches or to a ramp.

Routes

INDIAN ISLAND CIRCUMNAVIGATION: Moderate. The total paddling distance is eleven miles. Time your trip for high tide at the causeway, whether you start there or not. An effective plan for this trip is to launch at the wayside west of the causeway just after high tide and then head north into Kilisut Harbor. Starting off to the north gets you across the extensive tideflats of the harbor at high water. (The Oak Bay beach is not nearly such a long carry at lower water when you return.) Then, time your progress paddling north so as to catch the ebb current out of Kilisut Harbor at Fort Flagler State Park. Aim for either the slack or the beginning of the south-flowing flood current in the Port Townsend Canal.

If you catch the tide level at the causeway just right, you can ride the current through one of the two four-foot-wide culverts under the highway. Be careful! The current through here is fast. Be sure you will have enough headroom and enough water to avoid hanging up on the rocks at either end. But if you opt for discretion instead of this little thrill, the carry over the highway is easy.

Indian Island is an interesting blend of attractive "forbidden fruit" (restricted government property) surrounded by accessible public lands. Most of the island is occupied by the Naval Undersea Warfare Engineering Station, which stores ships' ammunition (reportedly nonnuclear). There are piers and buildings along the northwestern shore, but the remainder of the shoreline is remarkably pristine. The Navy employs a wildlife biologist to manage the island's habitat, and the station recently won national honors in a Department of Defense conservation award for its management.

However, *landings within the station boundaries are strictly prohibited*. Around the piers at Walan Point, it is forbidden to approach within six hundred feet. Nonetheless, cruising along the station's shorelines is a pleasant interlude with a largely undisturbed environment, and there are plenty of other places to stretch your legs. Look for river otter along the rocky shores.

The southern end of Indian Island, on both sides, has interesting sandstone formations with embedded nodules of harder rock that have eroded into studded surfaces, some forming tiny bridges like handles. Look for these south of Bishops Point on the Kilisut Harbor side and just north of the Port Townsend Canal on the west side.

Mystery Bay Recreation Area is the first chance for a shore stop, about two miles north of the causeway. There are toilet and picnic facilities, and a nearby store at Nordland.

FORT FLAGLER STATE PARK LOCAL PADDLING: Protected. The paddling distance is as desired. Fort Flagler has picnic facilities, bathrooms with running water, and a concession stand that sells snacks during the summer months. This area is popular for short paddling in the warmer protected waters. The western edge of the harbor is a low sandspit covered with grass and connected to the park at low tide. Called Bird Island locally, it is a popular place for large groups of seals to haul out at its southern end. Paddling out through the channel, you may find yourself surrounded by fifty or more of them.

Port Townsend Canal has currents of up to 3 knots. There are shore eddies except between the jetties at the south end, where you will have no choice but to fight the current if it is against you. Fairly large

Indian Island's sandstone nodules.

rips (standing waves) can form at either end depending on the current directions, which may be dangerous to kayakers not experienced with rough water.

Adjoining the southern end of the canal are Oak Bay County Park on the west side and Indian Island County Park on the east side. These have outhouses and picnic tables, and the sand-and-gravel tideflats are productive clamming areas.

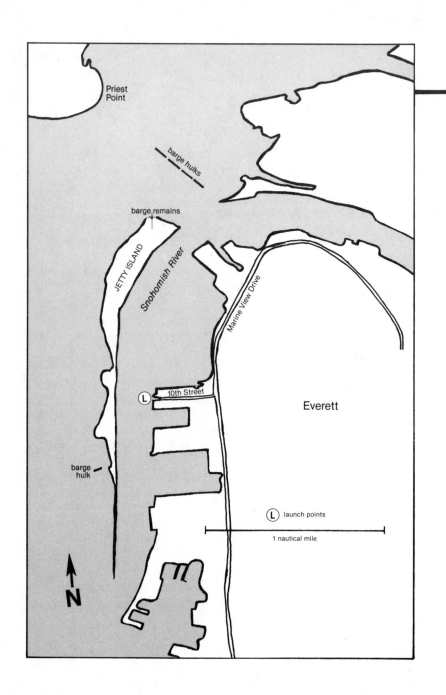

Priest
Point

barge hulks

barge remains

JETTY ISLAND

Snohomish River

Marine View Drive

10th Street

Everett

barge
hulk

Ⓛ launch points

1 nautical mile

N

Everett Harbor

Jetty Island and Vicinity

Just beyond the mills and marinas of Everett's waterfront, Jetty Island has both wildness and antiquity—seabirds and sea lions among rotting barges that were beached long ago to stabilize these shifting sandbars of the Snohomish River estuary. This is the closest opportunity for a solitary beach hike in the Seattle area (guaranteed in the winter months).

DURATION: Day trip only, two to four hours.

RATING: Protected.

CHARTS AND OTHER NAVIGATION AIDS: NOAA charts 18423 SC, 18441 (both 1:80,000), 18443 (1:40,000) or 18444 (1:10,000), and tide table.

PLANNING CONSIDERATIONS: Extensive tideflats make planning around the lower tides essential. The highest tides give access to small lagoons and backwaters on Jetty Island and make circumnavigation of the island shorter. Currents in the Snohomish River channels can be strong on either the ebb or flood tide.

Getting There and Launching

From Interstate 5, take Exit 193 (Pacific Avenue). Turn left under the freeway, and go about five blocks to Broadway Avenue. Turn right, and drive two blocks to Hewitt Avenue. Turn left and follow Hewitt through downtown Everett and downhill toward the waterfront. About three blocks short of the mill buildings on the shore ahead, turn right onto Marine View Drive. Follow this street for almost two miles, bearing left at the Y and railroad overpass, and passing the marina on the left. Turn left on 10th Street for the public launch and marine park. To launch use the launching ramps and the docks, or if they are very busy, the shoreline on either side. Note the closing hours for the park and be sure to return before then.

Route

JETTY ISLAND CIRCUMNAVIGATION: Protected. The total paddling distance is approximately four miles. Shorter excursions to northern Jetty Island and the vicinity are attractive in themselves. For the circum-

Winter fog along Jetty Island.

navigation, plan the direction in accordance with the Snohomish channel flow direction, which is stronger than on the west side of Jetty Island (the sequence here assumes a counterclockwise direction of travel).

From the launching ramp, follow the main Snohomish River channel upstream, passing extensive log storage facilities on the right. Across the channel is Jetty Island. This shore is used for log storage too, but less actively. At high tide you may be able to find routes behind the logs along the island's shore, winding through shallow passageways among rotting pilings and derelict, forgotten logs. Eventually, the water opens up to the left as you round the north end of Jetty Island.

The elevations of seabed and land hardly differ in this river outwash area. Jetty Island itself is hardly more than a long sandbar covered with salt grass, scotch broom, and an occasional tree. Over the years, wooden barges have been beached to control the movement of sand and silt. Walk inland toward the navigation marker tower at the north end of the island and you will find the old timbers and iron drift pins and bolts of barges that were beached and burned here long ago and are now completely surrounded by land.

Better-preserved barges are located about one-half mile north of Jetty Island. They are beached in a line that extends, along with countless pilings, most of the way across to the Tulalip shore to the north. If you appreciate wooden ships, they are worth the visit for a close look.

Beached barge hulks near Jetty Island.

These oceangoing vessels were wooden ships with all the workmanship that shipwrights of that era put into the more memorable sailing ships—diagonal triple planking, scarph joints, wooden treenail fastenings, and huge one-piece timbers no longer obtainable at any price.

The western edge of Jetty Island is an unbroken beach, with shallow waters warmed enough by the summer sun for a swim at high tide. At low tide, it becomes a sandy tideflat a mile or more wide. More hulks of old barges are found here and there along the beach.

A large colony of sea lions resides in this area during the late winter and spring (usually between February and May). At lower tides they move offshore, often floating in large somnambulant clusters. When the tide is in they like the beached barges or even the logs behind Jetty Island in Snohomish channel. Beware—they have little fear of humans and are apt to make threatening gestures to kayakers. (Many paddlers feel sea lions are potentially the most dangerous of all the marine mammals.)

The southern end of the island narrows to become a stone jetty for the last one-half mile. As currents may be strong against you for the paddle back upstream in the Snohomish River to the launching ramp, you may want to shorten the loop by portaging across the island north of the stone jetty—a distance of one hundred yards or less, depending on tides and logs stored on the east side.

Once in the river channel, you have the choice of following the wilder island shoreline or crossing to inspect the marina's fishboats and yachts. There are a variety of shops here with groceries, food, and spiritous beverages.

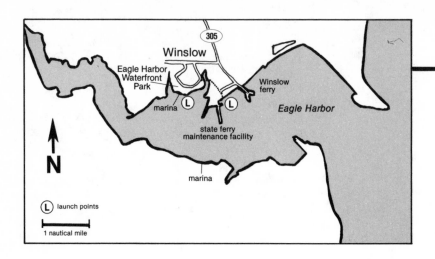

Eagle Harbor

This excursion is for kayakers who love all boats and things associated with the marine industry, all on Seattle's doorstep yet far from the urban bustle.

DURATION: Day trip only, one to three hours.

RATING: Protected.

CHARTS AND OTHER NAVIGATION AIDS: NOAA charts 18445 SC (1:80,000 with 1:25,000 Eagle Harbor inset) or 18449 (1:25,000), and tide table.

PLANNING CONSIDERATIONS: Higher tides allow exploration of the back bay and side coves in Eagle Harbor, which dry at lower tides.

Getting There and Launching

From the Winslow ferry dock, turn left at the first traffic light onto Winslow Way (turn right if coming south on Highway 305) into downtown Winslow. After one-tenth of a mile, turn left onto Bjune Drive, and then go another one-tenth of a mile to Eagle Harbor Waterfront Park.

There is public parking for Eagle Harbor Waterfront Park at the intersection of Koko Drive, as well as a short distance down Koko Drive. Beyond the latter is an unpaved road leading down to just above the gravel beach. For foot passengers with boats arriving on the Seattle ferry, see table 2 in the Appendix for directions for walking to the nearest launch points.

Route

EAGLE HARBOR EXPLORATION: Protected. Route and distance are as desired. From Eagle Harbor Waterfront Park, there are things to see in any direction. Just east are the state ferries' maintenance facilities, where out-of-service ferries dock. Here is a chance for a close-up look at the old veterans and super ferries. Before approaching them, look carefully for activity suggesting that one of them may be about to move.

Boats and a floathouse anchored in Eagle Harbor.

Two marinas, one directly across from the ferry docks and the other just west of the park, hold a wide assortment of fantastic yachts as well as unusual boats or barges that have been converted into live-aboards. Eagle Harbor also is popular with boaters (some of them live-aboards) who prefer to anchor out, thus avoiding any mooring fees. These are concentrated in the middle third of the harbor, and include floathouses on barges or rafts, old tug- and fishboats, and yachts.

Along shore are active industries (including a plant that produces treated pilings at the harbor entrance) and many relics from the past—sheds and warehouses on pilings, some abandoned and some still in use. A tiny, shallow cove across from the ferry dock is particularly pictur-esque for its old shoreline structures as well as its seclusion.

The very back of the harbor is less developed and less popular with boats, because it dries on lowest tides, but worth exploration if the tide is in. Midway back is an old warehouse dock that is a remnant of the berry farming industry that once thrived in the vicinity. It now houses small woodworking and sign-making shops and an insulation firm. Boat owners lease space for a variety of building and repair projects on the surrounding grounds.

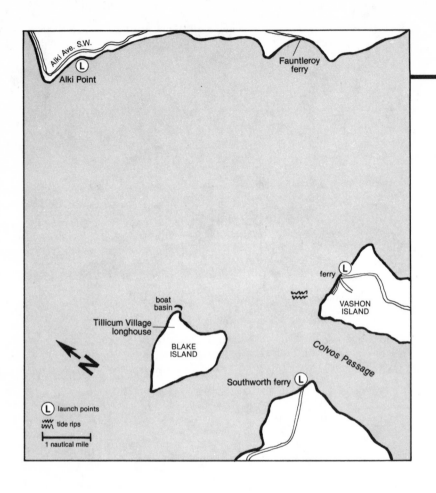

Blake Island

Come here for either a pleasant day trip or one of the most unusual kayak-camping experiences on Washington shores. Pitch your tent, take a shower in the heated rest room, and stroll over to the longhouse for a salmon dinner followed by Indian dancing. Too civilized for you? Then choose the more primitive facilities elsewhere on this state park island.

DURATION: One to two days.

RATING: Exposed, Moderate, and Protected.

CHARTS AND OTHER NAVIGATION AIDS: NOAA charts 18445 SC or 18448 (both 1:80,000), and 18449 (1:25,000). *Tide Prints* is helpful for planning (see Useful Publications).

PLANNING CONSIDERATIONS: Call ahead if you want a salmon dinner at Tillicum Village. (See route description for specifics.)

Getting There and Launching

For Alki Point launches, exit the West Seattle Freeway to Harbor Avenue Southwest and follow it north and around Duwamish Head, where it becomes Alki Avenue Southwest. Continue to Alki Point. For access via the ferry to Vashon Island or Southworth, follow the West Seattle Freeway and signs to the Fauntleroy ferry.

To launch from Alki Point, use a variety of spots either north or south of Alki Point Light Station where there is access to the stony beach below the bulkheads along Alki Avenue Southwest. Find on-street parking nearby (which may be difficult to do on sunny summer weekends).

To launch from Vashon Island, use the small ramp just east of the ferry dock. Parking next to the ramp is private, so unload and move cars as soon as possible to the ferry parking lot up the hill. This launch is difficult during high tides on the slippery, decaying ramp. During lower tides use the beach next to the ramp. Do not try to get to the beach from west of the ferry dock—this is private land.

To launch from Southworth, park in the ferry parking lot just east of the dock, and follow a short path from the lot to the sandy beach.

Routes

ALKI POINT TO BLAKE ISLAND: Exposed. The paddling distance is over three miles each way across open water with heavy shipping traffic. Currents in this area usually are less than 1 knot; they are strongest on the ebb. Be prepared to use one of the alternate routes and to return to West Seattle by ferry if the weather takes a turn for the worse.

VASHON ISLAND TO BLAKE ISLAND: Moderate. The paddling distance is approximately one and one-half miles each way, with about one and one-quarter miles across open water. Currents in this area rarely exceed 1 knot, but rips can occur between the two islands, particularly near the Allen Bank off Vashon Island. Colvos Passage is unique in that the current flows only on the ebb (setting north), and becomes weak and variable at other stages of the tide. Hence, this area becomes roughest on northerly winds when the ebb current opposes it.

SOUTHWORTH TO BLAKE ISLAND: Protected. The paddling distance is approximately one mile each way, with about three-quarters of a mile across open water. Currents here are weak and variable as long as you stay west of Colvos Passage and head for the more westerly shore of Blake Island.

Blake Island is roughly triangular, with a paddling circumference of about five miles. Most of this shoreline consists of low bluffs above rocky beach, but there are sandy beaches and a shallow high-tide lagoon at the west end. Ashore, an extensive network of paths and trails interconnect on the island.

There are three camping areas. On the western end of the island are sites with water (shut off during winter months) and rest rooms. There is no fee for camping there. On the southern shore is another free and more primitive site, which I have found to be muddy and exposed during the off-season. The eastern point is the most developed and is crowded with both boaters and boat-in campers during the summer months. A breakwater encloses a boat basin with floats for the boaters who come here year-round. The campground is between the boat basin and the stony beach to the south. (Land on this beach unless there is a strong southerly wind and waves, otherwise use the beach in the boat basin.) Most of the campsites have little or no southerly wind protection. There is a $3.00 fee between May and the beginning of September.

Between the campground and boat basin are heated rest rooms with showers ($.25 for six minutes). Nearby are semienclosed shelters for group picnics, which also can be used for cooking and shelter during the day if not already reserved. A large central fireplace can make them cozy in cooler weather.

The campground and beach at Blake Island's eastern point.

The most interesting element in this cluster is Tillicum Village longhouse, featuring Indian-style baked salmon followed by demonstrations of traditional dance. The clientele is primarily people arriving by tour boat from Seattle, but boaters may reserve a place for themselves by signing up at the longhouse at least one hour prior to mealtime. During the summer, service is daily at $13.00 for a meal and dances. During the off-season, the longhouse is open on weekends, and the cost is lower. Call 1-(206)-329-5700 for meal times and other information.

Places to Go— South Puget Sound

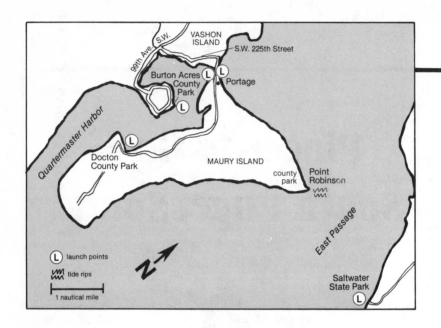

VASHON
ISLAND

99th Ave. S.W.

S.W. 225th Street

Burton Acres
County
Park

Portage

Docton
County Park

Quartermaster Harbor

MAURY ISLAND

county
park

Point
Robinson

East Passage

Ⓛ launch points

〰 tide rips

1 nautical mile

N

Saltwater
State Park

Maury Island

This trip combines the quiet charm of Quartermaster Harbor with a more challenging paddling area on the island's south coast to produce a circumnavigation that will leave you feeling as though you have seen a great deal as well as gotten a good day's exercise. Alternatives offer more relaxed dabbling in the harbor or a more demanding crossing from the mainland which includes shipping lanes and possible tide rips.

DURATION: Day trip only, up to eight hours. There are no camping facilities.

RATING: Protected, Moderate, and Moderate +.

CHARTS AND OTHER NAVIGATION AIDS: NOAA charts 18445 SC, 18448 (both 1:80,000) or 18474 (1:40,000), and current and tide tables.

PLANNING CONSIDERATIONS: Windy weather can make the east side of Maury Island unpleasant; the shallow beaches make offshore seas here steep and landings wet and rough. Plan for high tide to make the portage and avoid the extensive tideflats on the Quartermaster Harbor side.

Getting There and Launching

To reach Vashon Island, take Exit 163 from Interstate 5 and follow the West Seattle Freeway. In West Seattle, this becomes Fauntleroy Way and leads to the Fauntleroy ferry terminal. Exit the ferry at Vashon Island and drive south to the town of Vashon. To reach Maury Island and Quartermaster Harbor from the town of Vashon, follow 99th Avenue Southwest about three miles to Southwest 225th Street, where you turn left for Maury Island. For Burton Acres County Park, continue ahead on 99th Southwest to South 240th, turn left and then right onto Bayview Road. For Dockton County Park, continue past Portage on the Dockton-Portage Road about three and one-half miles.

Portage is the popular beginning and end for island circumnavigations. There usually is plenty of parking along either of the two roads that cross the isthmus, which are connected by Southwest 222nd Street. The carrying distance between high-tide lines is approximately two hun-

Robinson Point on Maury Island.

dred yards. A high-tide launch or take-out on the Quartermaster Harbor side is particularly desirable, since it dries to a large mud flat. A store (which a faded sign identifies as Lavender's, after a retired previous owner) is open year-round and has plenty of snacks and some groceries.

Quartermaster Harbor—either Burton Acres or Dockton county parks—provides easy access to sand and gravel beaches and plenty of parking.

To reach Saltwater State Park from Interstate 5, take Exit 149 (Kent-Des Moines). Turn left on Pacific Highway, then right onto South 240th Street, and finally right onto Marine View Drive. Follow Marine View Drive for approximately one mile to the entrance to the park on the right.

Saltwater State Park has easy access to a sand and gravel beach, though the parking lot may fill quickly on summer weekends.

Routes

QUARTERMASTER HARBOR: Protected. The paddling distances are as desired. Quartermaster Harbor is a fine place for a leisurely paddle year-round; for the warm waters and an opportunity for a swim during the summer, or for the quiet of one of those still, overcast days in November. The Burton peninsula effectively breaks up the fetch, so seas are unlikely to develop extensively. Either Burton Acres or Dockton county parks is a good place for a picnic, though Dockton offers more shoreside seclusion with its longer beach. Tables and rest rooms are available at both.

MAURY ISLAND CIRCUMNAVIGATION: Moderate. The total paddling distance is twelve miles. The long shallow bight of Maury Island's south side is an unusual mix of wildness amid the development of the central Puget Sound area. Though about one-half of the shoreline is occupied by residences, the remainder is grassy or wooded bluffs that invite a climb for a magnificent view of East Passage, Commencement Bay, Tacoma, and Mount Rainier in the distance. A large part of this shoreline and the bluffs behind are occupied by gravel and sandpits. I found that these did not detract from the attractiveness or interest of the area at all. Though some are operating, most are closed, and the pits are rapidly being reclaimed by grass, alder, and madrona. Rusty derelict conveyer systems descend through the brush to rotting terminals where barges once loaded. There are no public uplands or tidelands along this shore, so respect private property rights.

The south and north shores of Maury Island can turn into rough paddling in southerly or northerly winds, so you might want to plan a

An old gravel pit pier on Maury Island's southern shore.

circumnavigation to cover the portion most exposed to prevailing winds early in the day. Likewise, plan to avoid Point Robinson when the currents are contrary to the wind, as heavy tide rips can develop off the point. Also watch out for ship wakes on the beach.

The beach at Point Robinson and the grassy area behind the Coast Guard's lighthouse are open to the public during the day only. Up the hill northwest of the light is a county park also restricted to use during the day only.

SALTWATER STATE PARK TO POINT ROBINSON: Moderate +.

The total paddling distance is five miles. The crossing from Saltwater State Park, about two miles long at the narrowest point, is easy in moderate weather. Currents in the area are listed as weak and variable, though they do accelerate as water is compressed around Point Robinson. Rips are possible. The primary hazard on this crossing is marine shipping bound to and from Tacoma. The traffic lanes separate to either side of the midchannel buoy; northbound ships pass to the west. Wakes from ships and the many pleasure boats that ply this channel can create quite choppy seas. I also encountered surf at Point Robinson from a passing ship's wake that was nothing less than outer Pacific coast magnitude—look well before landing or launching, particularly at Point Robinson where ships pass close by.

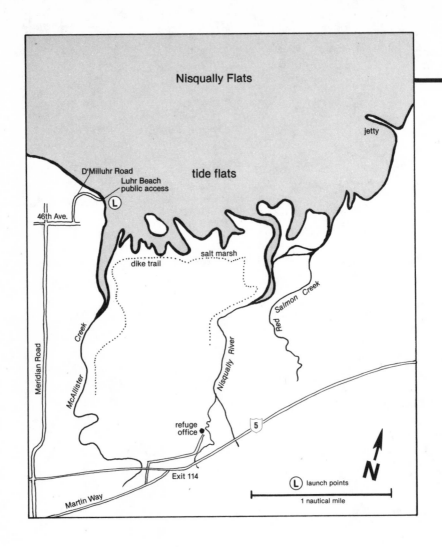

Nisqually Delta

This is one of the finest estuaries in Puget Sound, and a good place for kayakers who like to exploit their craft's shallow water abilities and explore brackish back channels as few other boaters can. Needless to say, this is *the* prime place for birders.

DURATION: Day trip only, two to four hours.

RATING: Protected.

CHARTS AND OTHER NAVIGATION AIDS: NOAA chart 18445 SC (1:80,000) and tide table.

PLANNING CONSIDERATIONS: Most channels are negotiable at midtide or above; high tide opens up many others. A Department of Game conservation license decal is required to use the Luhr Beach Public Access site. This area can be unpleasant in wind because of steep seas in the shallows and the chance of getting wet at the unprotected launch site. Waterfowl hunters are present in the state game portions of the delta from mid-October to mid-January.

Getting There and Launching

From Interstate 5, take Exit 114 (Nisqually). Just south of the freeway, turn right on Martin Way and follow it for just under one mile to Meridian Road. Turn right here and follow it for almost three miles to 46th Avenue. Turn right again and go one-quarter of a mile to D'Milluhr Road (unsigned) to the left (a sign points to public fishing). Follow this downhill for about one-half mile to the parking area.

The Department of Game's ramp at Luhr Beach has a moderate-size lot and beach next to the ramp for launching. At high tide there is limited launching space on the rocky beach, which becomes sandy at lower tides and offers more space. Note that a state game conservation license is required to park here and to use the state tidelands in the delta area. Next to the parking area is the Audubon Society's Nature Center, which is open on selected days of the week depending on the season.

Nisqually flats and Mount Rainier from Luhr Beach.

Route

NISQUALLY DELTA EXPLORATION: Protected. Route and distance are as desired. This area is managed by the U.S. Fish and Wildlife Service and the Washington Department of Game. The federal Nisqually National Wildlife Refuge includes the lower delta's tideflats and the meadows and woods of old farmland in the central portion above the dike that extend between McAllister Creek on the west and the Nisqually River on the east. State game lands include most of the lower salt marshes and most of the lands along McAllister Creek.

If you arrive near high tide, you may wish to explore the myriad channels that wander across the salt marshes in the lower delta. At highest tides you may be able to pick your way through shallow channels near the dike, though a spring tide is required to make it all the way across the delta by this inner route. Otherwise, head north to the lower flats to find your way to the eastern side of the delta, where you can head upstream in the Nisqually River or explore the connecting channel to Red Salmon Creek farthest to the east. At the very northeast corner of the flats (and still within federal refuge boundaries) is a sand jetty with old pilings and a beached barge that makes a nice lunch and sunbathing stop.

If you care to venture inland, McAllister Creek at the western edge of the delta offers the possibility of many miles of small stream paddling, using the last of the flood tide to assist you on the way in and then riding the ebb back out. The creek can be paddled easily to well inland of the freeway overpass.

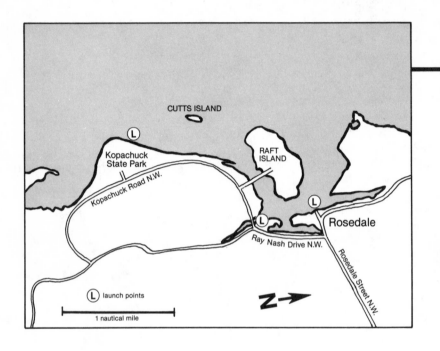

CUTTS ISLAND

RAFT
ISLAND

Kopachuck
State Park

Kopachuck Road N.W.

Rosedale

Ray Nash Drive N.W.

Rosedale Street N.W.

Ⓛ launch points

1 nautical mile

N→

Carr Inlet

Raft Island, Cutts Island, and Kopachuck State Park

If you live south of Seattle, this is an easy, short trip. It is ideal for those with limited saltwater experience or for families. Distances between stopovers are short. There are plenty of shore attractions and beaches with warm water for wading and swimming during the summer months. The route can be altered or shortened if weather is inclement.

DURATION: Day trip only, one to four hours. There are no camping facilities near the water.

RATING: Protected.

CHARTS AND OTHER NAVIGATION AIDS: NOAA charts 18445 SC or 18448 (both 1:80,000), 18474 (1:40,000), and tide table.

PLANNING CONSIDERATIONS: Consult a tide table before starting out, as minus tides make for very long carries to launches in the Rosedale area and may cut off access behind Raft Island.

Getting There and Launching

From Highway 16 in Gig Harbor, take the Gig Harbor City Center exit (this and other subsequent turns have signs for Rosedale and Kopachuck State Park). Turn left over the highway, then right after one-half mile on Hunt Street Northwest, and then right again onto 46th Avenue Northwest. After a mile, turn left at the intersection onto Rosedale Street Northwest and follow it for two and one-half miles to Rosedale.

To launch from Rosedale Street Northwest in Rosedale, approach the store and gas station in Rosedale, but go straight where the road curves left, passing a Dead End sign and a playground on the right. Drive about two blocks (you will pass a church on the left) and launch at the street's end onto a gravel beach. There is little room for more than one boat at a time to launch here at high tide when the beach is inun-

Cutts Island.

dated. Parking is a bit limited near the street's end, so avoid blocking private residences and park farther down the street if you have more than one vehicle.

For the Island View Market, follow the above instructions for Rosedale only turn left on Ray Nash Drive Northwest and drive three-quarters of a mile to the market. To launch from the Island View Market carry boats down the stairs to the right of the store and launch from the dock beyond (avoid the lowest tides, as this area dries). The carrying distance is approximately one hundred yards, with about thirty feet of vertical distance. The fee for launching and parking is $2.00. The store carries a small grocery and snack selection.

For Kopachuck State Park, follow the above instructions for Rosedale only turn left on Ray Nash Drive Northwest and drive three-quarters of a miles to Island View Market and then go straight over the bridge onto Kopachuck Road Northwest. Another one and three-quarters mile brings you to the park entrance.

To launch from Kopachuck State Park, you must carry your boat approximately one-third mile from the parking lot to the beach. Follow a gravel service road (which is smooth enough for boat carts) to the beach.

Routes

ROSEDALE VIA RAFT ISLAND, CUTTS ISLAND STATE PARK, AND KOPACHUCK STATE PARK LOOP: Protected.
The round-trip paddling distance is four miles.

Raft Island is exclusively residential, with gorgeous homes and moored yachts well worth the rubbernecking. What looks like a good launching beach on the Raft Island side of the bridge is not: it is restricted to use by island residents only.

Tiny Cutts Island seems larger than it really is. Steep bluffs, which increase in height toward the south end, partition the use of the island to either strolls in its madrona-and-fir woods above or a beach hike below. At the north end is a pebble-and-shell spit that extends almost to Raft Island during the lowest tides; this is steeper and easier on boats than the rockier beaches to the south. A pit toilet is located in the woods near the south end. This attractive little island cannot sustain camping or fires, and both are prohibited.

Kopachuck State Park, barely one-half mile from Cutts Island, brings you back to the intensity of land-access recreation. On a warm sunny day there are picnickers along the beach and kids splashing in the water. End the day here with a barbecue at one of the shoreside picnic sites.

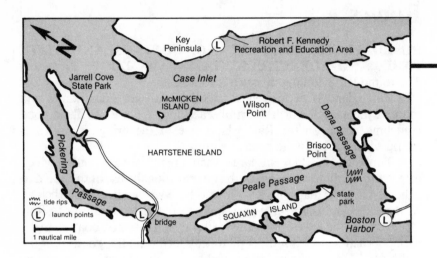

Key
Peninsula ⓛ   Robert F. Kennedy
              Recreation and Education Area

Jarrell Cove
State Park   *Case Inlet*

              McMICKEN
              ISLAND   Wilson
                             Point

                                        Dana Passage

Pickering   HARTSTENE ISLAND   Brisco
                                        Point

                             Peale Passage

〰〰 tide rips   state
ⓛ launch points   park

SQUAXIN ISLAND   *Boston
                           Harbor* ⓛ

Passage   ⓛ bridge

├──────┤
1 nautical mile

Hartstene Island

This island and its smaller neighbors are probably the most popular kayak destinations in south Puget Sound. They offer a fairly lengthy circumnavigation or alternatives for shorter day or overnight trips. There is a higher than usual concentration of parklands well spaced along this route.

DURATION: Day trip to three days.

RATING: Moderate + to Protected.

CHARTS AND OTHER NAVIGATION AIDS: NOAA charts 18445 SC or 18448 (both 1:80,000), and current tables.

PLANNING CONSIDERATIONS: There are no particular constraints for this area.

Getting There and Launching

Hartstene Island sits astride a portion of Puget Sound where myriad places to go are separated by only a few miles of water and thus easily accessible by boat but hours apart by highway. So too with the three launch suggestions for this area.

To begin your trip from the Olympia area use Boston Harbor. Drive Interstate 5 to Olympia, take Exit 105B (Plum Street) in Olympia. Drive north after exiting the freeway, and the rest of the route is essentially straight ahead. After passing through several intersections for approximately one mile, there will be water on the left. This road is East Bay Drive, which eventually becomes Boston Harbor Road. Continue another seven miles to 73rd Avenue Northeast and turn left. The ramp and parking lot are one-quarter mile beyond.

To launch from Boston Harbor, use the public ramp next to Boston Harbor Marina. The paved parking lot across the street from the ramp is public and usually has ample parking available. The marina store has basic beer-snacks-and-cigarettes fare.

To begin your trip from the Key Peninsula, use the Robert F. Kennedy Recreation and Education Area. Drive from Highway 302 in Key Center and follow the Gig Harbor-Longbranch Road south through Home. About one mile south of Home, turn right on Whiteman Road (there are signs for RFK here and at the next junctions). After another mile, bear left at the fork, and then turn right a little less than one-half mile beyond onto Bay Road. This road turns to gravel and then forks; take the right-hand road and follow it downhill to the recreation area.

The Robert F. Kennedy Education and Recreation Area (DNR operated) could serve as a starting point or as a campsite during the Hartstene Island circumnavigation. Generally, there is ample parking in an unpaved lot just above the beach. However, I was told that RFK users tend to be particularly boisterous, and that this is not a secure place to park a car and that I might return to find my car "better ventilated than it had been." (See route description on page 139 for camping information.)

To begin your trip from the Shelton area use the access near the Hartstene Island bridge. Turn onto Pickering Road from Highway 3 about eight miles north of Shelton (there is a sign for Hartstene Island). Follow this road approximately five miles to the bridge. The county's public ramp, dock, and parking lot are located just north of the bridge's western end. There is parking for about twenty vehicles in the lot near the ramp. This is a good midday starting point with about four miles of paddling south to camping at Squaxin Island State Park or the same distance north to Jarrell Cove State Park.

Routes

HARTSTENE ISLAND CIRCUMNAVIGATION: Moderate. The total paddling distance is twenty-three miles. Depending on the starting point, this route is well suited for a moderate-distance weekend trip, with an overnight stop at Jarrell Cove State Park. It could be extended to a leisurely two-night excursion with overnight stops at McMicken Island State Park, Robert F. Kennedy Education and Recreation Area, or Squaxin Island State Park.

The fastest currents on this route are encountered in Dana Passage at Hartstene Island's southern end—over 2 knots on the ebb, which is stronger than the flood current here. Planning with the current is especially important here, and eddies to assist against the current are unlikely along the shore.

Hartstene Island's shoreline between Brisco and Wilson points is for the most part natural, with an occasional house peeking over the high bluffs and tortuous stairways descending to the beach.

On the Key Peninsula across Case Inlet from Wilson Point is Robert F. Kennedy Education and Recreation Area. This DNR area is well visited by both overnight campers and day users, to the point that much of the area is bare and dusty. A float (in place during the summer)

Robert F. Kennedy Recreation and Education Area.

makes a lunch stop here convenient. Camping at RFK is most appealing during the off-season. There is one site near the water next to the launching ramp and other more distant ones to either the left or the right up the hill. Water and pit toilets are available.

The Key Peninsula shoreline north of RFK is pleasantly natural, with a pebble beach below high bluffs, the remains of an old pier, and a shallow lagoon with water that warms to bathtub temperatures during the summer and, at upper tidal stages, a miniature tide race at its entrance. Beach asparagus (glasswort) grows in profusion at the upper tide line.

Hartstene Island's shore offers a similar setting. Buffingtons Lagoon, less than one mile south of McMicken Island, is another pleasant stop, and the lagoon is accessible to kayaks only and only at high tide.

McMicken Island State Park is particularly attractive to paddlers who like undeveloped campsites and isolation. A pit toilet is the only facility on shore. Landings and access to the island are practical only on the southwest side due to steep bluffs above a narrow beach elsewhere. Behind this pebble-and-shell beach is a meadow affording the handiest campsites. The fenced-in area and buildings are private land. A trail network circles through the dense forest north of the meadow, with occasional views out over the bluffs. Be alert for poison oak. In the forest are a few camp clearings that would be the best all-weather campsites in spite of the long hauling distances from the beach. Fires are not allowed on the island, so bring a camp stove.

Developments become more numerous on the Hartstene Island

shoreline north of McMicken Island, so plan on Jarrell Cove as your next stop—five miles beyond. Though the tidelands one mile north of McMicken Island are public DNR property, there is no other public access before Jarrell Cove.

Though Jarrell Cove is developed and popular with both boaters and motorists during the summer season, this tiny harbor is a jewel, particularly the narrow inlet extending eastward from the cove. The state park campground rarely fills even during the busy months. Kayakers would find it particularly attractive during the less busy off-season because of the amenities: easy water access for camping, running water in the bathrooms, and pleasant campsites.

There is a $6.00 fee for camping, though a few primitive campsites are available for a lower fee of $3.00. These are just above the first float encountered on the left as you enter the cove. One site, located just beyond the float, has its own access from the beach, is the most private, and provides snug weather protection. The remainder of the campground sites are above the bluff in a meadow (approximately one hundred yards up a smooth gravel pathway).

Jarrell Cove Marina, directly across from the state park's outer

The beach on McMicken Island.

float, has a small grocery open year-round (the only one on Hartstene Island).

West of Jarrell Cove, Hartstene's shore again becomes wild, inviting high-tide paddling close to shore, where trees overhang the steep banks providing tunnellike paddling and some shelter from headwinds. Currents in Pickering Passage and Peale Passage beyond rarely exceed 1 knot, so you should have little trouble advancing along shore at any stage of the tide. (Currents are strongest under the Hartstene Island bridge.)

Once in Peale Passage, the shore of Squaxin Island is a fine oasis of natural beauty. Paddling close to its shore, it is easy to imagine yourself exploring Puget Sound two centuries ago with British explorer Captain Vancouver. With the exception of the state park, Squaxin Island is an Indian reservation (*do not go ashore without permission*), and its east shore has escaped development except for an oyster-rearing operation in the bay midway down the island. Occasional decaying shacks are the only evidence of the sparse settlement. More evident residents are river otter, blue heron, or even a coyote trotting along the beach.

Squaxin Island State Park, a little more than two nautical miles away on the southeast side of the island, is one of the most popular destinations for kayakers in the area, especially for day trippers out of Boston Harbor. There is a dock at the mouth of the shallow cove and ample campsites in a strip of lawn that extends along the beach to the south for about one-quarter mile. All sites provide easy access for boats and gear, and those farthest from the dock are likely to offer the most privacy. A $3.00 camping fee is collected via the self-registration station near the dock. A park ranger is intermittently present during the summer season. Water is not available. A new solar-composting toilet augments the pit toilets.

BOSTON HARBOR TO SQUAXIN ISLAND STATE PARK: Moderate +. The round-trip paddling distance is approximately five miles. According to local park rangers, this is a very popular trip for people trying kayaks for the first time, with potentially disastrous results. Dana Passage currents can attain more than 2 knots, and rips can be lively here, especially with an opposing wind. The weakest currents are encountered by crossing directly from Boston Harbor to Squaxin Island. This route, however, involves crossing two miles of open water. In unsettled weather, take the route that follows close to the shore east from Boston Harbor, and then cross Dana Passage to Brisco Point on Hartstene Island when currents are slack or in agreement with the wind. Then follow Hartstene Island's west shore north to opposite the Squaxin Island State Park before crossing to Squaxin Island. (See Hartstene Island circumnavigation p. 138 for state park particulars.)

A camp group launching kayaks at Squaxin Island State Park.

ROBERT F. KENNEDY RECREATION AND EDUCATION AREA TO MCMICKEN ISLAND STATE PARK: Moderate. The round-trip paddling distance is approximately five miles. (See Hartstene Island circumnavigation p. 138 for route and destination particulars.)

HARTSTENE ISLAND BRIDGE TO JARRELL COVE STATE PARK: Protected. The round-trip paddling distance is eight miles. The strongest currents are in the vicinity of the bridge. (See Hartstene Island circumnavigation p. 138 for route particulars.)

HARTSTENE ISLAND BRIDGE TO SQUAXIN ISLAND STATE PARK: Protected. The round-trip paddling distance is approximately eight miles. (See Hartstene Island circumnavigation p. 138 for route particulars.)

Appendices

Table 1 CALCULATING CURRENTS USING NOAA'S TABLES

The example shown is for June 3, 1985, a day of particularly strong currents, at San Juan Island's Limestone Point (see Stuart Island chapter). In the lower portion of the table, corrections for Limestone Point (Spieden Channel) are based on daily predictions for San Juan Channel (the upper portion of the table). One hour is added to the calculations for daylight saving time. To calculate the first slack for Limestone Point, take the slack water time for San Juan Channel (A), minus the correction time for the minimum current before the ebb at Limestone Point (B), plus one hour for daylight saving time (DST).

0328 – 100 (1 hour 0 minutes) + 100 (DST) = 0328.

To calculate the maximum ebb current for Limestone Point, take the maximum current time for San Juan Channel (C), plus the maximum ebb current correction for Limestone Point (D), plus one hour for daylight saving time (DST).

0724 + 026 (minutes) + 100 (DST) = 0850.

To calculate the speed in knots for that time, take the maximum current velocity for San Juan Channel (E), multiplied by the ebb speed ratio for Limestone Point (F).

4.3 × 1.2 = 5.2.

To calculate when the next slack for Limestone Point will occur, take the next slack water time for San Juan Channel (G), minus the correction time for the minimum current before the flood for Limestone Point (H), plus one hour for daylight saving time (DST).

1047 + 023 (minutes) + 100 (DST) = 1210.

Note that the interval of this large exchange is almost nine hours. Though the afternoon flood current will be 5 knots in San Juan Channel, Spieden Channel will be slower than during the morning ebb. To calculate the speed in knots for that time, take the maximum current velocity for San Juan Channel (I), multiplied by the flood speed ratio for Limestone Point (J).

5.0 × 0.7 = 3.2.

Table 1   145

SAN JUAN CHANNEL (south entrance), WASHINGTON, 1985

F-Flood, Dir. 010° True   E-Ebb, Dir. 180° True

JUNE

Day	Slack Water Time	Maximum Current Time	Vel.
	h.m.	h.m.	knots
1 Sa	0214 0922 1630 2210	0555 1237 1910	4.2E 4.6F 2.5E
2 Su	0250 1004 1726 2309	0024 0639 1325 2004	2.0F 4.3E 4.9F 2.5E
3 M	0328 **A** 1047 **G** 1819	0113 0724 **C** 1415 2057	1.6F 4.3E **E** 5.0F **I** 2.5E

CURRENT DIFFERENCES AND OTHER CONSTANTS, 1985

NO.	PLACE	TIME DIFFERENCES				SPEED RATIOS	
		Min. before Flood	Flood	Min. before Ebb	Ebb	Flood	Ebb
		h. m.	h. m.	h. m.	h. m.		
	SAN JUAN CHANNEL	on SAN JUAN CHANNEL, p.58					
1655	Cattle Point, 1.2 miles southeast of....	+0 11	-0 20	+0 34	-0 01	0.3	0.9
1660	SAN JUAN CHANNEL (south entrance).......	Daily Predictions					
1665	Kings Point, Lopez Island, 1 mile NNW of	+0 51	-0 07	+0 27	+0 36	0.6	0.5
1670	Pear Point, 1.1 miles east of..........	+0 40	+1 09	-0 10	+1 01	0.4	0.5
1675	Turn Rock Light, 1.9 miles northwest of.	+1 19	+1 22	+0 20	-0 01	0.4	0.5
1680	Crane Island, south of, Wasp Passage....	-0 10	+0 35	+0 29	+0 07	0.2	0.1
1685	Wasp Passage Light, 0.5 mile WSW of.....	+0 19	+0 28	+0 15	-0 15	0.5	0.4
1690	Spring Passage, south entrance..........	+0 04	-1 09	-0 43	-0 13	0.4	0.4
1695	Limestone Point, Spieden Channel........	+0 23**H**	-0 12	-1 00**B**	+0 26**D**	0.7**J**	1.2**F**

Table 2 LAUNCH POINTS NEAR WASHINGTON STATE FERRY TERMINALS

Ferry Terminal	Launch Point	Carrying Distance from Ferry
Seattle	Public floats, foot of Washington Street.	300 yards
Winslow	First street on left after parking lot; go 75 yards, turn left on path to beach, *or* turn right on path over footbridge to Eagle Harbor Waterfront Park.	300 yards 500 yards
Bremerton	Port of Bremerton dock at foot of 1st Street, north of terminal.	100 yards
Edmonds	Public beach north of terminal.	200 yards
Kingston	Beach north of terminal; go over guardrail then down embankment to path to beach.	300 yards
Port Townsend	Beach south of terminal.	200 yards
Keystone	Fort Casey State Park beach or launch ramp south of terminal.	150 yards
Mukilteo	State park south of terminal.	300 yards
Fauntleroy	Public access north of terminal.	250 yards
Vashon	Old ramp south of terminal.	150 yards
Southworth	Beach east of terminal; follow exit route in parking lot to the left, double back around fence.	400 yards
Anacortes	Beach south of terminal; follow path from parking lot.	150 yards
Lopez Island	No public access at terminal. The trail and beach west of parking lot is private land.	
Shaw Island	Beach west of terminal.	50 yards
Orcas Island	Russell's floats, west of terminal, $5 fee.	75 yards
Friday Harbor	Public dock north of terminal; use loading or dinghy floats.	250 yards

Equipment Checklist

KAYAK EQUIPMENT

Paddle(s) and spare
Flotation bags (if no bulkheads)
Bilge pump or bailing container
Sponge
Spray skirt(s)
Life jacket(s)

SAFETY AND NAVIGATION EQUIPMENT

Flares or smoke devices
Compass
Nautical charts and chart case
Current and tide tables
Weather radio or VHF
  transceiver
Rescue equipment (paddle-float
  bag, stirrup, etc.)
Towline
Repair kit

PERSONAL EQUIPMENT

Full change of clothing
Paddling jacket
Foul-weather jacket
Rain pants
Wool hat
Shoes for walking on shore
Sun hat
Sunglasses with leash
Sunscreen
Flashlight

Knife
First-aid kit
Water container
Toilet paper
Insect repellent
Fishing gear and license
Binoculars
Camera
Wet or dry suit (if desired)
Waterproof storage bags

CAMPING EQUIPMENT

Money (one-dollar bills for state
  park camping fees)
Tent
Tarp
Sleeping bag
Sleeping pad
Fire starter
Lighter or waterproof matches
Stove
Fuel container
Raccoon-proof food storage
  containers
Cooking pots
Personal eating items
Dish-washing items
Personal hygiene items
Waterproof storage bags
Tote bag(s)

Useful Publications

Canadian Hydrographic Service. *Current Atlas: Juan de Fuca Strait to Strait of Georgia.* Ottawa: Canadian Hydrographic Service Department of Fisheries and Oceans, 1983.

This atlas provides the most accurate and detailed information on tidal currents in this complex region. For a given hour and tidal range, the user is directed to a chart showing currents at that time. Calculations required to arrive at the correct chart make this resource a bit difficult to use. (See *Washburne's Tables* for a simplified method of finding the proper current chart.)

Cummings, Al, and Bailey-Cummings, Jo. *Gunkholing in the San Juans.* Edmonds, Washington: Nor'westing (No date).

This boater's guide includes a lot of local lore not found elsewhere. It is written in a friendly and entertaining style.

Department of Natural Resources, State of Washington. Public tideland booklets: *North Puget Sound,* 1978; *San Juan Island Region,* 1985; *South Puget Sound,* 1978; *Strait of Juan de Fuca,* 1984.

These booklets are handy for identifying public tidelands and DNR upland picnic or camping facilities. The tidelands are primarily of interest for shellfish gathering or just a place to stretch your legs at low tide. They are of little use to you when the tide is high because the uplands are usually private. The booklets are available by writing to:

Photos, Maps, and Reports
Capitol Park Building
1063 South Capitol Way AW-11
Olympia, WA 98504
(206) 753-5338

Evergreen Pacific. *Shellfishing Guide: Washington Waters.* Seattle: Straub Printing & Publishing, 1981.

This guide identifies public shorelines and parks for all of the state's coastal waters. Some information is dated, and there are omissions and inaccuracies (Orcas Island's Point Doughty DNR Recreation Area is misspelled, misidentified as a county park, and mislocated to Waldron Island).

Island Canoe Company. *Current and Tide Tables for Puget Sound, Deception Pass, the San Juans, Gulf Islands, and Strait of Juan de Fuca.* Bainbridge Island, Washington: Island Canoe Company, published annually.
This collection of local tide and current information is otherwise available only in large NOAA volumes.

————. *The New San Juan Current Guide Including the Gulf Islands and Strait of Juan de Fuca.* Bainbridge Island, Washington: Island Canoe Company, 1985.
The charts in this publication show currents with correction factors for local slack times and speeds.

————. *Puget Sound Current Guide.* Bainbridge Island, Washington: Island Canoe Company, 1984.
This publication includes the same information for Puget Sound as found in the above publication.

Lilly, Kenneth E., Jr. *Marine Weather of Western Washington.* Seattle: Starpath School of Navigation, 1983.
Lilly's book provides some of the most helpful information ever for understanding the patterns and idiosyncrasies of western Washington's weather and learning about how weather features happen. It is essential if you want to go beyond just listening to forecasts for weather prediction, and it also includes useful information on waves.

McGary, Noel, and Lincoln, John W. *Tide Prints: Surface Tidal Currents in Puget Sound.* Seattle: University of Washington Press, 1977 (out of print).
This book, with its separate charts showing currents at different points in the tide cycle, complements the Canadian Hydrographic Service's *Current Atlas: Juan de Fuca Strait to Strait of Georgia.* Unfortunately, the book is out of print at this writing. Check local libraries for a copy.

Mueller, Marge. *The San Juan Islands Afoot and Afloat.* 2d ed. rev. Seattle: The Mountaineers, 1983.

Mueller, Marge, and Mueller, Ted. *South Puget Sound Afoot and Afloat.* Seattle: The Mountaineers, 1983.

These two companion volumes provide comprehensive coverage of each area; just about any place worth mentioning is included. They also include good information about facilities and services on shore.

Saltwater Access Map. Snohomish, Washington: Snohomish Publishing Co., 1984.
  Primarily oriented toward launch and marina facilities for fishermen, this map is helpful for spotting put-ins and take-outs. The information on public upland facilities (e.g., camping) is spotty.

Tidelog: Puget Sound Edition. Tiburon, California: Pacific Publishers, published annually.
  This is a useful combination of tide and current information for the year. It provides daily tidal curves that show slacks and associated current strengths and lunar and solar phases as they affect tides. It also includes current charts for Puget Sound and current tables for Deception Pass.

U.S. Department of Commerce, National Oceanic and Atmospheric Administration. *Tidal Current Tables: Pacific Coast of North America and Asia.* Washington, D.C.: Government Printing Office, published annually.
  This volume includes current information for local points throughout the Northwest, as well as the rest of the Pacific coast. See Island Canoe Company publications if you are interested in Washington's inland waters only.

Washburne, Randel. *The Coastal Kayaker: Kayak Camping on the Alaska and B.C. Coast.* Seattle: Pacific Search Press, 1983.
  Though primarily oriented toward the Southeast Alaska and British Columbia coasts, *The Coastal Kayaker* offers trip information for Puget Sound and the San Juan Islands that is not covered in this book. It also includes basic information for getting started in sea kayaking.

Washburne's Tables. Bellevue, Washington: Weatherly Press, published annually.
  Use these tables in conjunction with the helpful Canadian Hydrographic Service's *Current Atlas: Juan de Fuca Strait to Strait of Georgia.* These tables provide direct access to the proper current chart at any hour of any day without need for calculations or adjustment for daylight saving time.

Index

Boldface numerals indicate pages on which maps appear.

After drop, 19–20
Aleutian Low, 17–18
Alki Point to Blake Island, 118
Alternative routes, 43

Beaches in winter, 49
Birds and birding, 39, 66, 95, 129.
  See also individual birds
Blake Island, **116**–19
Blakely Island, circumnavigation of,
  85–87
Boston Harbor to Squaxin Island
  State Park, 141
Bracing, 30

Camping, 36–38
  minimum impact, 38–39
  winter, 50
Carr Inlet, **132**–35
Charts, 41
Clamming, 104
Clark Island via Gooseberry Point
  and Lummi Island, 62
Clothing, for off-season, 50
Cormorants, pelagic, 66
CPR (cardiopulmonary resuscitation),
  20
Craft Island, 96–97
Current Atlas (Canadian Hydro-
  graphic Service), 26, 27, 53, 62–63,
  67, 71, 90
Currents, 23–31
  calculation of, 144

hazards from, 26–30
prediction of, 25–26
*Current Tables for the Pacific Coast
  of North America and Asia*
  (NOAA), 25
Cypress Island, **88**–92
circumnavigation of, 90–92

Daily distance, 43
Daily tide cycle, 24
Department of Natural Resources
  (DNR) Recreation Areas, 35–36
Dry suits, 19, 50
Dumping surf, 49

Eagles, 39, 66, 97
Eagle Harbor, **112**–14
Eddies, 28–30
  and upstream progress, 30–31
Equipment
  checklist, 147
Everett Harbor, **106**–10

Fatalities, 14, 27
Ferries, 45–47
Fires, 37
Fog, 18
Food
  purchasing, 48
  storage of, 38
Forecasts, 19
Fort Flagler State Park, 103–4

Gales, 17

Hartstene Island, **136**–42

Boston Harbor to Squaxin Island
State Park, 141
circumnavigation of, 138–41
Hartstene Island Bridge to Jarrell
Cove State Park, 142
Hartstene Island Bridge to Squaxin
Island State Park, 142
RFK Recreation Area to McMicken
Island State Park, 142
Hazards
from currents, 26–30
marine traffic, 20–22
Hydraulic head, 25
Hypothermia, 19–20

Indian Island, **100**–4
circumnavigation of, 102–3
Fort Flagler State Park, 103–4
Island Canoe Company, 25–26

Jetty Island
circumnavigation, 108–10

Kayaks
limitations of, 11–12
towing, 12

La Conner to Goat Island, 97–99
Launching and parking, 47–48
Launch points near Washington
State ferry terminals, 146
Lilly, Kenneth, *Marine Weather of
Western Washington*, 17
Lincoln, J. W., *Tide Prints*, 26
Loading boats, 42
Lummi Island, **70**–73
circumnavigation of, 72–73

Marine traffic hazards, 20–22
Marine weather, 17–19
*Marine Weather of Western Wash-
ington* (Lilly), 17
Maury Island, **122**–26

circumnavigation of, 125–26
Quartermaster Harbor, 124–25
Saltwater State Park to Point
Robinson, 126
McAllister Creek, 131
McGary, N., *Tide Prints*, 26
Minimum impact camping, 38–39

National Parks and Wildlife Refuges,
33–34
Nautical charts, 41
Nisqually Delta, **128**–31
NOAA, 25–26, 41
broadcasts of, 19
North Beach
to Point Doughty to Patos Island
to Clark Island to Lawrence
Point, 63–68
to Sucia Island, 62–63
Northern Rim Islands, **60**–68

Off-season paddling, 48–50
Orcas Island, winds around, 18

Pacific High, 17–18
Pacific Northwest boating, 9–14
Paddling off-season, 48–50
Parking, 47–48
Parks and Recreation Areas, 33–36
Pelagic cormorants, 66
Predicting currents, 25–26
Public Lands, 33–36
Puget Sound
North, 93–119
South, 121–42

Quartermaster Harbor, 124–25

Raccoons, 37–38
Radio, 19
Ranges, 29–30
Ratings of routes, 13–14, 44–45
Red-tailed hawks, 97

Reid Harbor
  Prevost Harbor via Johns Pass
    loop, 57
  Prevost Harbor via Turn Point
    loop, 57–58
Rips, 27–30
River otters, 103
Roche Harbor, San Juan Island to
  Stuart Island, 55–57
Rosario Strait, Western, **82**–87
Rosedale via Raft Island, Cutts
  Island State Park and Kopachuck
  State Park, 135
Routes, rating of, 13–14

Saltwater State Park to Point
  Robinson, 126
San Juan Islands, 51–58
  Central, **74**–80
Sea breezes, 18
Sea Kayaker magazine, 27, 63, 91
Sea lions, 110
Seals, 38–39, 65, 103
Shaw Island, circumnavigation of,
  76–80
Shipping routes, 20–22
Shoreline, importance of, 9–10
Skagit River Delta, **94**–99
  Craft Island, 96–97
  La Conner to Goat Island to
    Delta, 97–99
Solitude, 38
Southworth to Blake Island, 118–19
Squaxin Island, 141
Standing waves, 29
Stoves, 37
Stuart Island, **52**–58
Surf, dumping, 49

Tide cycle (daily), 24
Tide Prints (McGary and Lincoln),
  26
Tides, 23–31

rips, 27–30
Tillicum Village Longhouse, 119
Traffic lanes, 20–21
Transits, 29–30
Trips
  choosing, 43–44
  planning, 41–43
  ratings of, 44–45

Vashon Island to Blake Island, 118
VHF transceiver, 19, 21

Washburne's Tables, 26
Washington State Ferries, 45–47
Washington State Parks, 34–35
Water supply, 36–37
Water temperature, 19–20
Waves, 27–29
Weather
  allowances and alternative routes,
    43
  marine, 17–19
  off-season, 49–50
Wet suits, 19
Wooden ships, 109–10

Other Books from Pacific Search Press

COOKING

American Wood Heat Cookery (2d Ed. Revised & Enlarged)
    by Margaret Byrd Adams
The Apple Cookbook by Kyle D. Fulwiler
The Bean Cookbook: Dry Legume Cookery by Norma S. Upson
The Berry Cookbook (2d Ed. Revised & Enlarged)
    by Kyle D. Fulwiler
Canning and Preserving without Sugar (Updated)
    by Norma M. MacRae, R.D.
The Eating Well Cookbook by John Doerper
Eating Well: A Guide to Foods of the Pacific Northwest
    by John Doerper
The Eggplant Cookbook by Norma S. Upson
A Fish Feast by Charlotte Wright
Food 101: A Student Guide to Quick and Easy Cooking
    by Cathy Smith
One Potato, Two Potato: A Cookbook by Constance Bollen
    and Marlene Blessing
River Runners' Recipes by Patricia Chambers
The Salmon Cookbook by Jerry Dennon
Shellfish Cookery: Absolutely Delicious Recipes from the
    West Coast by John Doerper
Starchild & Holahan's Seafood Cookbook by Adam Starchild
    and James Holahan
Wild Mushroom Recipes by Puget Sound Mycological Society
The Zucchini Cookbook (3d Ed. Revised & Enlarged)
    by Paula Simmons

CRAFTS

The Chilkat Dancing Blanket by Cheryl Samuel
The Guide to Successful Tapestry Weaving by Nancy Harvey
An Illustrated Guide to Making Oriental Rugs
    by Gordon W. Scott
Patterns for Tapestry Weaving: Projects and Techniques
    by Nancy Harvey
Spinning and Weaving with Wool (Updated) by Paula Simmons

HEALTH

A Practical Guide to Independent Living for Older People
  by Alice H. Phillips and Caryl K. Roman

NATURE

The Birdhouse Book: Building Houses, Feeders, and Baths
  by Don McNeil
Growing Organic Vegetables West of the Cascades
  by Steve Solomon
Marine Mammals of Eastern North Pacific and Arctic Waters
  edited by Delphine Haley
Seabirds of Eastern North Pacific and Arctic Waters
  edited by Delphine Haley

NORTHWEST SCENE

At the Forest's Edge: Memoir of a Physician-Naturalist
  by David Tirrell Hellyer
The Pike Place Market: People, Politics, and Produce
  by Alice Shorett and Murray Morgan
Seattle Photography by David Barnes
They Tried to Cut It All by Edwin Van Syckle

OUTDOOR RECREATION

*Cross-Country Downhill and Other Nordic Mountain Skiing
  Techniques* (3d Ed. Revised & Enlarged) by Steve Barnett
The Coastal Kayaker: Kayak Camping on the Alaska and B.C. Coast
  by Randel Washburne
Derek C. Hutchinson's Guide to Sea Kayaking
  by Derek C. Hutchinson
River Runners' Recipes by Patricia Chambers
*The White-Water River Book: A Guide to Techniques,
  Equipment, Camping, and Safety*
  by Ron Watters/Robert Winslow, photography
*Whitewater Trips for Kayakers, Canoeists, and Rafters in
  British Columbia, Greater Vancouver through Whistler
  and Thompson River Regions* by Betty Pratt-Johnson
*Whitewater Trips for Kayakers, Canoeists, and Rafters on
  Vancouver Island* by Betty Pratt-Johnson

TRAVEL

Alaska's Backcountry Hideaways: Southcentral
    by Roberta L. Graham
Alaska's Southeast: Touring the Inside Passage
    (2d Ed. Revised & Enlarged) by Sarah Eppenbach
Cruising the Columbia and Snake Rivers (2d Ed. Revised &
    Enlarged) by Sharlene P. and Ted W. Nelson and Joan LeMieux
Cruising the Pacific Coast, Acapulco to Skagway (4th Ed. Revised)
    by Carolyn and Jack West
The Getaway Guide I: Short Vacations in the Pacific Northwest
    (2d Ed. Revised & Enlarged) by Marni and Jake Rankin
The Getaway Guide II: More Short Vacations in the Pacific
    Northwest (2d Ed. Revised & Enlarged)
    by Marni and Jake Rankin
The Getaway Guide III: Short Vacations in Northern California
    by Marni and Jake Rankin
The Getaway Guide IV: Short Vacations in Southern California
    by Marni and Jake Rankin
Journey to the High Southwest: A Traveler's Guide
    (2d Ed. Revised) by Robert Casey

PACIFIC SEARCH PRESS will send you books directly if your bookstore does not have what you want!

Quantity	Title	Price	Amount
	THE COASTAL KAYAKER: KAYAK CAMPING ON THE ALASKA AND B.C. COAST, Washburne	$10.95	
	DEREK C. HUTCHINSON'S GUIDE TO SEA KAYAKING, Hutchinson	$12.95	
	WHITEWATER TRIPS: VANCOUVER ISLAND, Pratt-Johnson	$8.85	
	ALASKA'S BACKCOUNTRY HIDEAWAYS: SOUTHCENTRAL, Graham	$10.95	
	Washington State residents add 7.9% sales tax		
	Postage and handling		$ 1.50
	TOTAL ORDER		

☐ Send me a free catalog of Pacific Search Press titles.

I have enclosed payment of $_____.

I wish to use my credit card.

MasterCard number _____ Expiration date _____

VISA number _____ Expiration date _____

Name _____

Address _____

City_____ State _____ Zip _____

Payment must accompany order.

All orders are sent fourth class book rate. Please allow 3 to 6 weeks for delivery.

SATISFACTION GUARANTEED! If not completely satisfied, return the book(s) to us within 10 days of receipt for a full refund.

PACIFIC SEARCH PRESS
222 Dexter Avenue North
Seattle, Washington 98109
(206) 682-5044